CATCH-UP
MATH

Get your child back on track!

Whole Numbers ◎ Addition ◎ Subtraction

Multiplication ◎ Division ◎ Fractions

Data Tables ◎ Graphs ◎ Measurement

Classifying Shapes ◎ Time

Publishing Credits

Corinne Burton, M.A.Ed., *President* and *Publisher*
Emily R. Smith, M.A.Ed., *SVP of Content Development*
Véronique Bos, *Vice President of Creative*
Lynette Ordoñez, *Content Manager*
Avery Rabedeaux, *Assistant Editor*
Kevin Pham, *Graphic Designer*

Image Credits: all images from iStock, Dreamtime, and/or Shutterstock

Standards

© Copyright 2010 National Governors Association Center for Best Practices and Council of Chief State School Officers. All rights reserved.
© Copyright 2007–2023 Texas Education Agency (TEA). All Rights Reserved.
© 2023 TESOL International Association
© 2023 Board of Regents of the University of Wisconsin System

A division of Teacher Created Materials

5482 Argosy Avenue
Huntington Beach, CA 92649
www.tcmpub.com/shell-education
ISBN 979-8-7659-7155-0
© 2024 Teacher Created Materials, Inc.

This Edition is for sale in North America (including Canada) only.
From material first published and copyright Pascal Press.

Printed by: **418**
Printed in: **USA**
PO#: **PO9308**

CONTENTS

CONTENTS

ABOUT CATCH-UP MATH

The **Catch-Up Math** series enables children to start from scratch when they are struggling with grade-level math. Each book takes math back to the foundation and ensures that all basic concepts are consolidated before moving forward. Lots of revision and opportunities to practice and build confidence are provided before moving on to new topics.

Each new topic is introduced clearly with simple explanations, examples, and trial questions (with answers) before children move to the Practice section. To help students understand difficult topics, instructional videos are included throughout the book.

This book has 13 chapters that cover a variety of mathematical concepts. The chapters are:

SCAN to watch video

A QR code on a topic page provides access to the video.

1	Whole Numbers	8	Length
2	Addition	9	Shapes
3	Subtraction	10	Area
4	Multiplication	11	Capacity
5	Division	12	Mass
6	Fractions	13	Time
7	Data		

★ A review section that can be used as an assessment and to check children's progress is included at the end of each chapter.

★ Answers are at the back of the book.

How to Use This Book

Children can work through the pages from front to back or choose individual topics to reinforce areas where they are struggling.

The topics are introduced with:

- clear instructions, using simple language

- completed examples and incomplete examples for students to tackle before moving on to the **Your Turn** sections

- videos linked by QR codes to provide additional instruction and clarify difficult concepts

Each Your Turn section contains a SELF CHECK for students to reflect and give self-assessment on their understanding.

HOW TO USE THE QR CODES IN CATCH-UP MATH

A unique aspect of the Catch-Up Math series is the **instructional videos**.

The videos further explain and clarify various mathematical concepts. The videos are simply accessed via QR codes and can be watched on a phone or tablet. Or, view all the videos by following this link: tcmpub.digital/cu-math3.

Access the video by scanning the QR code with your device.

SCAN to watch video

Each video shows the page from the book. An instructor talks through the concepts and examples and demonstrates what children need to do. The solutions to the examples are presented before children tackle the Your Turn sections. This careful instruction ensures that children can confidently move on to the following Practice questions. Children should be encouraged to check their Your Turn answers before moving on.

25 instructional videos included!

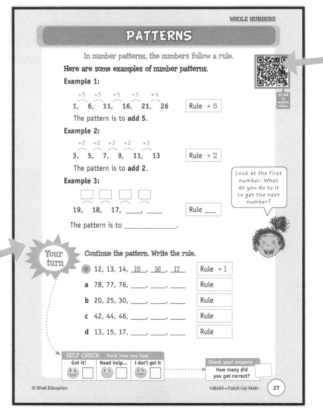

Scan this to access the video.

After watching the video, children can confidently complete the Your Turn section.

MATH SKILLS

This book contains key math skills from both second and third grade to help your child catch up to grade level.

Grade 2 Math Skills	Pages
Understand place value, including the values of the digits in three-digit numbers.	13–18, 29–32, 37–42, 51–52
Count up and down, between 0–1,000, by 2s, 5s, 10s, and 100s.	9–12, 19–26
Read and write numbers to 1,000 using numerals, words, and expanded form.	16–18, 39–40, 43–46
Compare the values of three-digit numbers using > (greater than), < (less than), and = (equal to), and write numbers in ascending and descending order.	33–36
Add and subtract numbers under 100.	70–73, 76–77, 80–81, 89–96, 99–100
Use objects (models) and drawings to add and subtract numbers under 1,000.	78–79, 82–83, 97–98, 101–102
Understand the relationship between addition and subtraction.	74–75
Use repeated addition to solve multiplication problems.	108–109
Use repeated subtraction to solve division problems.	126–127
Split objects and groups of objects into halves, quarters, eights, thirds, and fifths.	132–143
Organize and interpret data shown in tables, bar graphs, and picture graphs.	151–166
Measure the lengths of objects to the nearest whole unit (inches, feet, centimeters, meters, etc.).	170–178
Recognize and draw shapes. Identify triangles, quadrilaterals, pentagons, and hexagons.	181–186
Count the number of squares that cover an object to find its area.	188–191
Tell and write time from analog and digital clocks to the nearest five minutes.	222–230

MATH SKILLS (CONT.)

Grade 3 Math Skills	Pages
Understand place value, including the values of the digits in four-digit numbers.	53–59
Read and write numbers to 1,000 using numerals, words, and expanded form.	49–50, 55–57
Round numbers to the nearest 10, 100, or 1,000.	47–48, 60–61
Find and explain patterns in a series of numbers.	27–28
Add and subtract numbers under 1,000.	78–79, 82–83, 97–98, 101–102
Understand that multiplication problems represent groups multiplied by the number of objects in each group.	106–107
Apply properties of multiplication and division to multiply and divide numbers under 100.	110–113
Understand that division problems represent a total number of objects divided into groups.	116–125
Understand that fractions are parts of wholes.	132–143
Use knowledge of numerators (number of parts) and denominators (the whole) to write fractions.	132–143
Compare fractions and identify equivalent fractions.	144–146
Create and interpret tables, picture graphs, and bar graphs with scaled intervals.	151–166
Use data in graphs and tables to solve "how many more" and "how many less" problems.	151–166
Understand that shapes can be categorized based on their attributes (number of sides, number of parallel sides, etc.). Recognize rhombuses, rectangles, and squares as quadrilaterals.	181–186
Understand that a square with a side length of 1 unit is called a unit square.	192–193
Find the area of a rectangle by multiplying its length by its width.	194–195
Measure and estimate liquid volumes and masses of objects using metric units and customary units.	199–206, 210–217
Solve word problems involving volumes or masses that are given in the same unit.	212–217

WHOLE NUMBERS

Whole numbers are the counting numbers from 0 to infinity. Each whole number is made up of digits.

A single-digit number is a number that is made up of only one number (or digit).

| 0, 1, 2, 3, 4, 5, 6, 7, 8, 9 | ← Single-digit numbers |

Two-digit numbers are numbers made up of two numbers.

Example 1: 36

is a two-digit number because it is made up of two numbers, **3** and **6**.

Example 2:

Create a two-digit number using 7 and 4.

_____

Is your number of fingers a one- or two-digit number?

Your turn

Circle all the single-digit numbers in red and the two-digit numbers in blue.

0	62	28	4	43	37
7	8	99	5	17	74
6	89	9			

SELF CHECK   Mark how you feel

Got it!	Need help...	I don't get it

Check your answers

How many did you get correct?

PRACTICE

 Fill in the missing numbers.

1	2			5	6			9	10
		13	14			17	18		
21		23			26			29	
		33		35		37	38		40
41	42		44		46			49	
		53		55		57	58		
61			64		66			69	
	72			75			78		80
81		83			86			89	
			94			97			100

Look before   Look after

 Use the table in question 1 to answer these questions.

⬤ What number comes before 97?   96

a What number comes after 52?   _____

b What number comes before 37?   _____

c What number is 2 more than 44?   _____

d What number is 2 less than 87?   _____

e What number is 5 more than 36?   _____

f What number is 5 less than 21?   _____

g What number is 10 more than 76?   _____

h What number is 10 less than 41?   _____

3 Write the numbers from each box on the number line next to it.

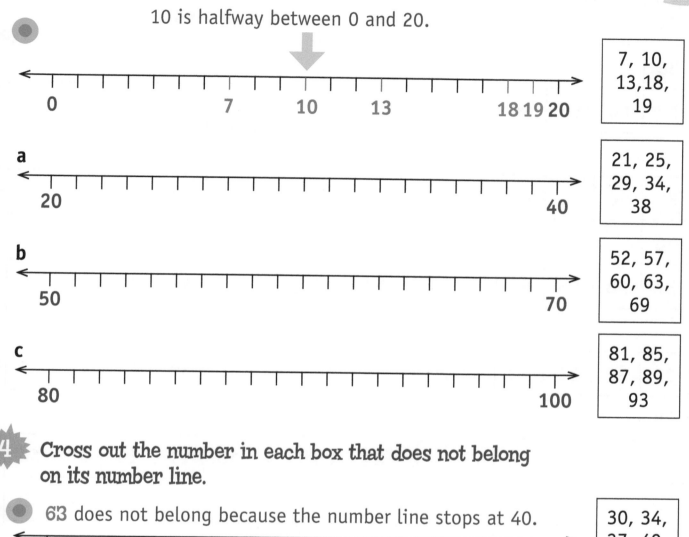

10 is halfway between 0 and 20.

7, 10, 13, 18, 19

a

21, 25, 29, 34, 38

b

52, 57, 60, 63, 69

c

81, 85, 87, 89, 93

4 Cross out the number in each box that does not belong on its number line.

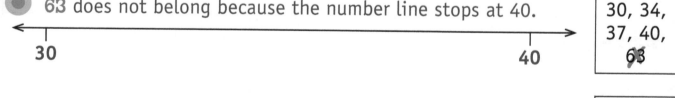

63 does not belong because the number line stops at 40.

30, 34, 37, 40, 63

a

21, 34, 38, 22, 48

b

59, 65, 73, 78, 80

c

43, 49, 51, 57, 64

Look at the path of numbers from 1 to 100.

89	90	91	92	93	94	95	96	97	98	99	100

88

87	86	85	84	83	82	81	80	79	78	77	76	75	74

73

59	60	61	62	63	64	65	66	67	68	69	70	71	72

58

57	56	55	54	53	52	51	50	49	48	47	46	45	44

(43)

29	30	31	32	33	34	35	36	37	38	39	40	41	42

28

27	26	25	24	23	2̶2̶	21	20	19	18	17	16	15	14

13

Start →	1	2	3	4	5	6	7	8	9	10	11	12

5 Circle in red the number BEFORE each of the numbers.

● 44 → 43 is circled in red because 43 comes before 44.

a 27		**d** 57		**g** 72
b 36		**e** 33		**h** 48
c 22		**f** 81		**i** 91

6 Put a blue X (✗) on the number AFTER each of the numbers.

● 21 → The number after 21 is 22, so an ✗ is on the number.

a 44		**d** 58		**g** 79
b 29		**e** 37		**h** 43
c 31		**f** 84		**i** 96

TENS AND ONES

Two-digit numbers (or tens) are the numbers from 10 to 99.

Numbers less than 10 are called ones.

Ones are also called units. They are one-digit numbers.

Example 1:

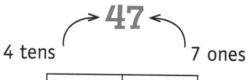

tens	ones
4	7

The number 4 has been put in the tens box because 47 has 4 tens.

The 7 is in the ones box because 47 has 7 ones.

If you make 47 using Base 10 blocks, it looks like this:

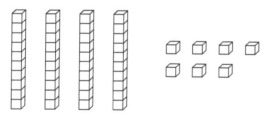

There are only nine one-digit numbers but lots of two-digit numbers.

Example 2: How many tens are in 89? _____

Your turn

Complete the table.

	Number	Tens	Ones	Base 10
	52	5	2	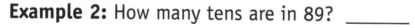
a	38			
b	26			

PRACTICE

 Color the tens and ones to match the number.

Number	Tens	Ones
37		
a 56		
b 24		
c 83		
d 97		
e 68		

2 Group the tens and ones.
Circle the tens in blue and ones in red.

⬤ 36 = __3__ tens and __6__ ones

   = __30__ + __6__

   = __36__

(X X X X X X X X X X)   (X X X X X X X X X X)

(X X X X X X X X X X)   (X X X X X X)X X X X

---

a 45 = ___ tens and ___ ones

   = ____ + ___

   = ____

○ ○ ○ ○ ○ ○ ○ ○ ○ ○
○ ○ ○ ○ ○ ○ ○ ○ ○ ○
○ ○ ○ ○ ○ ○ ○ ○ ○ ○
○ ○ ○ ○ ○ ○ ○ ○ ○ ○
○ ○ ○ ○ ○ ○ ○ ○ ○ ○

c 51 = ___ tens and ___ ones

   = ____ + ___

   = ____

☆ ☆ ☆ ☆ ☆ ☆ ☆ ☆ ☆ ☆
☆ ☆ ☆ ☆ ☆ ☆ ☆ ☆ ☆ ☆
☆ ☆ ☆ ☆ ☆ ☆ ☆ ☆ ☆ ☆
☆ ☆ ☆ ☆ ☆ ☆ ☆ ☆ ☆ ☆
☆ ☆ ☆ ☆ ☆ ☆ ☆ ☆ ☆ ☆
☆ ☆ ☆ ☆ ☆ ☆ ☆ ☆ ☆

---

b 27 = ___ tens and ___ ones

   = ____ + ___

   = ____

△ △ △ △ △ △ △ △ △ △

△ △ △ △ △ △ △ △ △ △

△ △ △ △ △ △ △ △ △ △

d 18 = ___ tens and ___ ones

   = ____ + ___

   = ____

✖ ✖ ✖ ✖ ✖ ✖ ✖ ✖ ✖ ✖

✖ ✖ ✖ ✖ ✖ ✖ ✖ ✖ ✖ ✖

EXPANDED NUMBERS

Expanded numbers are numbers written to show the value of each digit.

Example 1:   2 tens   3 ones

and

10 + 10   1 + 1 + 1

20   3   20 + 3 = 23

Example 2:   __ tens   __ ones

and

___ + ___ + ___ + ___   __ + __ + __ + __ + __ + __ + __

_____   _____ ___ + ___ = ___

> You can work out what a number is by seeing its expanded form.

Your turn — Complete the table.

	Base 10	Expanded form
38		30 + 8
a 16		
b 52		
c 67		
d 73		

SELF CHECK   Mark how you feel

Got it!   Need help...   I don't get it

Check your answers — How many did you get correct?

PRACTICE

1 Expand the numbers.

    16 = __10__ + __6__

    a 27 = ____ + ___

    b 59 = ____ + ___

    c 31 = ____ + ___

    d 44 = ____ + ___

    e 63 = ____ + ___

    f 19 = ____ + ___

    g 98 = ____ + ___

    h 84 = ____ + ___

    i 60 = ____ + ___

2 Fill in the missing spaces.

Number	Base 10		Expanded form
	Tens	Ones	
56	|||||	☐☐☐☐☐☐	50 + 6
a			70 + 2
b 97			
c	|||	☐☐☐☐	
d			80 + 5
e 13			
f			40 + 9
g	||	☐☐☐☐☐☐☐☐	

3 Write the number shown on each abacus.

63

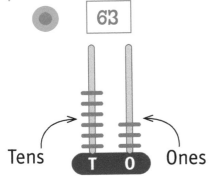

Tens   Ones

a ▢

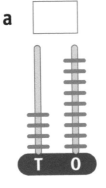

b ▢

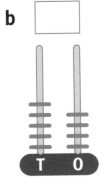

c ▢

d ▢

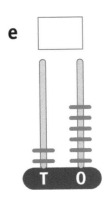

e ▢

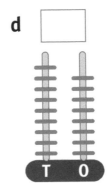

4 Draw lines on each abacus to show the tens and ones for the number below it.

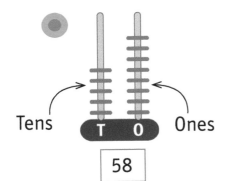

Tens   Ones

58

a

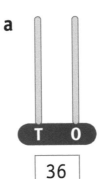

36

b

22

c

94

d

59

e

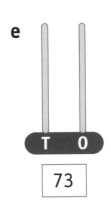

73

COUNTING BY TENS

When counting by tens, you only count every 10th number.

0   10   20   30   40   50   60   70   80   90   100
+10   +10   +10 +10 +10 +10 +10 +10 +10 +10

When counting by tens from 0, all the numbers end in 0
(the digit in the ones place is 0).

If you are counting by tens, but are starting from the number 6,
all the numbers end in 6 (the digit in the ones place will be 6):

6, 16, 26, 36, 46, 56, 66, 76, 86, 96.

If you count backward by tens, starting at 94,
all the digits in the ones place will be 4:

94, 84, 74, 64, 54, 44, 34, 24, 14, 4.

Example 1: Count forward by tens.

13, 23, 33, 43, 53, 63

Example 2: Count backward by tens.

108, 98, _____, _____, _____, _____

> Wherever you start from, the "gap" is always 10!

Your turn

Write the missing numbers.

10, 20, 30, 40, _50_, _60_, _70_

a 90, 80, 70, _____, _____, _____

b 3, 13, 23, _____, _____, _____

c 77, 67, 57, _____, _____, _____

SELF CHECK   Mark how you feel
Got it!   Need help...   I don't get it

Check your answers
How many did you get correct?

PRACTICE

1 Write the missing numbers.

⦿ 10, 20, __30__, __40__, 50, __60__

a 99, 89, _____, _____, 59, _____

b 24, 34, _____, _____, 64, 74

c _____, 40, _____, _____, 70, _____, _____

d 37, 47, _____, _____, 77, _____, _____

e 58, 68, _____, _____, _____, 108

2 Write the missing numbers.

⦿ ⟨16⟩ ⟨26⟩ ⟨36⟩ ⟨46⟩ ⟨56⟩ ⟨66⟩ ⟨76⟩ ⟨86⟩

a △ △77 △ △57 △47 △ △27 △

b [28] [ ] [48] [ ] [68] [78] [ ] [ ]

c ◯ ◯31 ◯ ◯ ◯61 ◯ ◯81 ◯91

d ⬡20 ⬡ ⬡40 ⬡ ⬡ ⬡ ⬡80 ⬡

e ▽12 ▽ ▽ ▽42 ▽52 ▽ ▽ ▽

f ◯93 ◯ ◯ ◯ ◯53 ◯ ◯ ◯

g ◯ ◯84 ◯74 ◯ ◯ ◯44 ◯ ◯24

© Shell Education

ODD AND EVEN NUMBERS

Odd numbers	Even numbers
If a number is ODD, it ends with a 1, 3, 5, 7, or 9.	If a number is EVEN, it ends with a 2, 4, 6, 8, or 0.
Some odd numbers: 33, 75, 97, 21.	Some even numbers: 30, 24, 78, 46.

Example 1: Is 34 an odd or even number?

3④ ← It ends in an even number.
So, 34 is an even number.

Is your number of fingers an odd number or an even number?

Example 2: Is 87 an odd or even number?

87 ← It ends in an _____ number.
So, 87 is an _____ number.

Your turn

Circle all the odd numbers with red and all the even numbers with blue.

25	72	48	40
39	93	16	57
	81	90	

SELF CHECK   Mark how you feel

Got it!	Need help...	I don't get it
☐	☐	☐

Check your answers
How many did you get correct?

PRACTICE

 1 Complete each sentence.

   a Even numbers end in 2, ___, ___, ___ or ___.

   b Odd numbers end in 1, ___, ___, ___ or ___.

 2 Write five even numbers between the numbers shown.

   ● 20 and 40   22, 24, 26, 28, 30 _____

   a 10 and 30   _____

   b 50 and 70   _____

   c 80 and 100   _____

   d 0 and 20   _____

 3 Write five odd numbers between the numbers shown.

   ● 40 and 60   41, 43, 45, 47, 49 _____

   a 70 and 90   _____

   b 0 and 20   _____

   c 50 and 65   _____

   d 20 and 45   _____

 4 Write the next three numbers.

   ● 86, 88, _90_, _92_, _94_   **e** 12, 10, ____, ____, ____

   a 52, 54, ____, ____, ____   **f** 24, 22, ____, ____, ____

   b 83, 85, ____, ____, ____   **g** 73, 71, ____, ____, ____

   c 91, 93, ____, ____, ____   **h** 90, 88, ____, ____, ____

   d 42, 44, ____, ____, ____   **i** 41, 39, ____, ____, ____

COUNTING BY TWOS

When counting by twos, you only count every second number.

Example 1:

This pattern counts even numbers by twos:

2, 4, 6, 8, 10, 12, 14, 16, 18, 20.

Example 2:

This one counts odd numbers by twos:

1, 3, 5, 7, 9, 11, 13, 15, 17, 19.

Look at the numbers in the ones place. What patterns can you see?

Example 3:

Count forward by twos.

24, 26, _____, _____, _____.

33, 35, _____, _____, _____.

Your turn

Count forward by twos.

42, 44, _46_, _48_, _50_, _52_, _54_

a 47, 49, _____, _____, _____, _____, _____

b 82, 84, _____, _____, _____, _____, _____

c 37, 39, _____, _____, _____, _____, _____

d 59, 61, _____, _____, _____, _____, _____

SELF CHECK   Mark how you feel
Got it!   Need help...   I don't get it

Check your answers
How many did you get correct?

PRACTICE

1 Complete the patterns.

2	4	6	8	10	12	14	16	18	20	22

a

80	78			72	70			64		

b

93	91			85		81	79			

c

32			38				46			

d

74				82	84			90		

2 Complete the tables.

2		6	8	
	14	16		
22			28	
				40
	44			
		56	58	
62				70
	74			
		86		90
	94		98	

Even numbers

1	3			9
11		15	17	
	23			
		35		
41			47	
	53	55		
61				69
		75	77	
	83		87	
91		95		

Odd numbers

COUNTING BY FIVES

When counting by fives, you only count every fifth number.

Example 1: Count forward by fives.

+5   +5   +5   +5   +5   +5   +5   +5   +5
5,   10,   15,   20,   25,   30,   35,   40,   45,   50

Example 2: Count backward by fives.

−5   −5   −5   −5   −5   −5   −5
85,   80,   75,   70,   65,   60,   55,   50

Look at the last digit in each number. What do you notice?

Example 3: Count forward by fives.

15, 20, ____, ____, ____, ____

Example 4: Count backward by fives.

65, 60, ____, ____, ____, ____

Your turn

Fill in the missing numbers.

● 25, 30, 35, _40_, _45_

a 0, 5, 10, ____, ____   **d** 65, 60, 55, ____, ____

b 35, 40, 45, ____, ____   **e** 20, 15, 10, ____, ____

c 75, 70, 65, ____, ____   **f** 40, 45, 50, ____, ____

SELF CHECK   Mark how you feel

Got it!	Need help...	I don't get it

Check your answers
How many did you get correct?

PRACTICE

 Fill in the missing numbers.

⬤ 10, 15, _20_, _25_, 30

a 35, ____, 45, ____, ____

b 55, ____, 45, ____, ____

c 100, ____, 90, ____, ____

d 70, 65, ____, ____, 50

e 85, ____, 75, 70, ____

f 40, ____, ____, 25, 20

 Fill in the missing numbers.

⬤ 50 — 55 — 60 — 65 — 70 — 75

a 25 — ◯ — 15 — ◯ — 5 — ◯

b 50 — 55 — ◯ — ◯ — 70 — ◯

c ◯ — 40 — ◯ — 30 — ◯ — 20

 Count by fives and color the numbers. The first two have been done for you.

1	2	3	4	5	6	7	8	9	10
11	12	13	14	15	16	17	18	19	20
21	22	23	24	25	26	27	28	29	30
31	32	33	34	35	36	37	38	39	40
41	42	43	44	45	46	47	48	49	50
51	52	53	54	55	56	57	58	59	60
61	62	63	64	65	66	67	68	69	70
71	72	73	74	75	76	77	78	79	80
81	82	83	84	85	86	87	88	89	90
91	92	93	94	95	96	97	98	99	100

PATTERNS

In number patterns, the numbers follow a rule.

Here are some examples of number patterns.

Example 1:

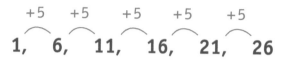

+5   +5   +5   +5   +5

1,   6,   11,   16,   21,   26

Rule + 5

The pattern is to **add 5**.

Example 2:

+2   +2   +2   +2   +2

3,   5,   7,   9,   11,   13

Rule + 2

The pattern is to **add 2**.

Example 3:

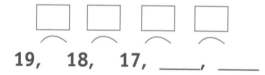

19,   18,   17, ____, ____

Rule ___

The pattern is to _____.

> Look at the first number. What do you do to it to get the next number?

Your turn

Continue the pattern. Write the rule.

● 12, 13, 14, _15_ , _16_ , _17_   Rule + 1

a 78, 77, 76, ____, ____, ____   Rule

b 20, 25, 30, ____, ____, ____   Rule

c 42, 44, 46, ____, ____, ____   Rule

d 13, 15, 17, ____, ____, ____   Rule

PRACTICE

1 Fill in the missing numbers. Write each rule.

● 60, 65, 70, __75__ , __80__ , __85__ | Rule + 5 |

a 75, 70, 65, ____, ____, ____ | Rule |

b 50, 60, 70, ____, ____, ____ | Rule |

c 27, 29, 31, ____, ____, ____ | Rule |

d 2, 4, 6, ____, ____, ____ | Rule |

e 94, 93, 92, ____, ____, ____ | Rule |

2 Cross out the number that does not belong.

● | 5 | 10 | 1̶2̶ | 15 | 20 | 25 |

a | 67 | 65 | 64 | 63 | 61 | 59 |

b | 30 | 35 | 38 | 40 | 45 | 50 |

c | 17 | 27 | 37 | 38 | 47 | 57 |

d | 40 | 45 | 50 | 55 | 58 | 60 |

e | 86 | 85 | 80 | 75 | 70 | 65 |

f | 64 | 65 | 66 | 68 | 70 | 72 |

3 Fill in the boxes.

●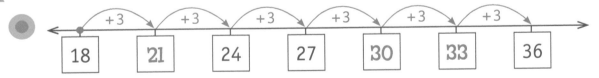

+3 +3 +3 +3 +3 +3

| 18 | 21 | 24 | 27 | 30 | 33 | 36 |

a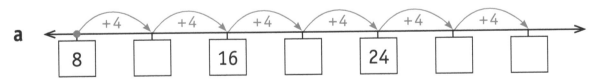

+4 +4 +4 +4 +4 +4

| 8 | | 16 | | 24 | | |

b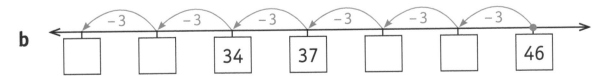

−3 −3 −3 −3 −3 −3

| | | 34 | 37 | | | 46 |

c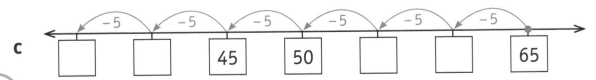

−5 −5 −5 −5 −5 −5

| | | 45 | 50 | | | 65 |

HUNDREDS

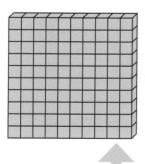

This Base 10 block has 100 cubes.

Numbers from 100 to 999 are three-digit numbers, or hundreds.

The number 326 is a three-digit number because it has three digits.

When you count by 100s, you only count every 100th number.

Example 1: Counting forward by 100s

+100   +100   +100   +100   +100

100, 200, 300, 400, 500, 600

Look at the first digit in each number. What do you notice?

Example 2: Counting backward by 100s

−100   −100   −100   −100   −100

600, 500, 400, _____, _____, _____

Your turn

1 Circle all the three-digit numbers.

(127)   73   328   21   425   16

42   408   5,201   25   4,378

2 Fill in the missing numbers.

a   100, _____, _____, 400, _____

b   800, _____, _____, 500, _____

SELF CHECK   Mark how you feel

Got it!   Need help...   I don't get it

Check your answers
How many did you get correct?

PRACTICE

 Match these.

Words	Base 10	Number
six hundred		200
a eight hundred		500
b five hundred		700
c two hundred		600
d seven hundred		800

 Fill in the missing numbers.

200, 300, _400_ , _500_ , 600

a 700, _____, 500, _____, _____

b 1,000, 900, _____, 700, _____, _____

c 600, _____, 800, _____, 1,000

d _____, 400, _____, 200, 100

e 100, _____, _____, 400, _____

 Match the words to the correct number.

four hundred   a one hundred   b eight hundred   c nine hundred

800   100   400   900

MODELING HUNDREDS

Hundreds can be shown in different ways.

Example 1:

Below is the number **523** in Base 10 blocks and on the abacus.

5 **hundreds**   2 **tens**   3 **ones**
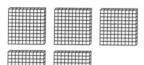 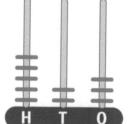

Example 2: Here is the number **164.** What is on the abacus?

1 **hundred**   6 **tens**   4 **ones**

Your turn

1 Color the Base 10 blocks to model the number.

● 124

a 245

2 What number is shown on each abacus?

● 352   **a** [   ]   **b** [   ]

 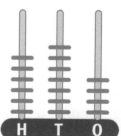 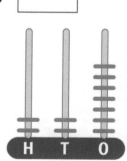

SELF CHECK   Mark how you feel
Got it!  [ ]   Need help... [ ]   I don't get it [ ]

Check your answers
How many did you get correct?

 PRACTICE

1 Write each number shown by the Base 10 blocks.

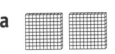

<u>4</u> hundreds   <u>2</u> tens   <u>1</u> one   = <u>421</u>

a

___ hundreds   ___ ten   ___ ones   = _____

b

___ hundreds   ___ tens   ___ ones   = _____

c

___ hundreds   ___ tens   ___ ones   = _____

d

___ hundreds   ___ tens   ___ ones   = _____

e

___ hundreds   ___ tens   ___ ones   = _____

2 Match each number with the correct abacus.

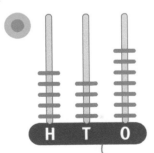   **a** 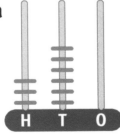   **b** 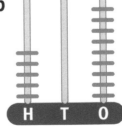   **c**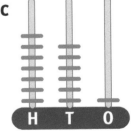

| 509 | 547 | 761 | 360 |

ORDERING THREE-DIGIT NUMBERS

You can order numbers from smallest to largest or largest to smallest.

SCAN to watch video

These three-digit numbers have been ordered from smallest to largest: 124, 238, 315.

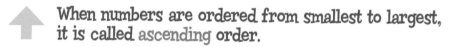 When numbers are ordered from smallest to largest, it is called ascending order.

These three-digit numbers have been ordered from largest to smallest: 357, 219, 103.

When numbers are ordered from largest to smallest, it is called descending order.

> Remember: "descending" has a d for down, so the numbers are going down.

Your turn

1 Write these numbers in ascending order.

● 241, 735, 422, 376   241, 376, 422, 735

a 903, 910, 924, 951   _____

b 425, 417, 302, 124   _____

c 127, 316, 240, 903   _____

2 Write these numbers in descending order.

● 784, 214, 224, 606   784, 606, 224, 214

a 411, 116, 215, 918   _____

b 317, 712, 545, 103   _____

c 102, 120, 210, 201   _____

SELF CHECK   Mark how you feel

Got it!	Need help...	I don't get it

Check your answers
How many did you get correct?

PRACTICE

 1 Order these numbers from smallest to largest.

⦿ 127, 129, 124   _124, 127, 129_

a 245, 249, 240   _____

b 425, 472, 427   _____

c 103, 130, 301   _____

d 603, 630, 613   _____

2 Order these numbers from largest to smallest.

⦿ 523, 502, 575   _575, 523, 502_

a 711, 749, 703   _____

b 104, 143, 140   _____

c 211, 219, 129   _____

d 316, 613, 136   _____

3 Write these numbers in ascending order.

⦿ | 667 | 756 | 823 | 149 | ➡ | 149 | 667 | 756 | 823 |

a | 217 | 479 | 987 | 418 | ➡ | | | | |

b | 848 | 979 | 656 | 242 | ➡ | | | | |

4 Put these numbers in descending order.
Write a **1** under the largest number and a **4** under the smallest.

⦿ 824   249   605   214
   [1]   [3]   [2]   [4]

b 711   909   439   999
   [ ]   [ ]   [ ]   [ ]

a 183   811   219   752
   [ ]   [ ]   [ ]   [ ]

c 707   615   421   103
   [ ]   [ ]   [ ]   [ ]

SMALLEST AND LARGEST THREE-DIGIT NUMBERS

| 8 | 4 | 9 | Here are the digits 8, 4, and 9.

By moving them around, I can make the smallest number possible for these three digits.

| 4 | 8 | 9 | I put the 4 in first position as it has the least value. Then the 8, then the 9.

The smallest three-digit number I can make is 489.

If I move the numbers around again, I can make the largest number possible.

| 9 | 8 | 4 | I put the 9 in first position as it has the greatest value. Then the 8, then the 4.

The largest three-digit number I can make is 984.

> Practice counting in order so you know which digits have the greatest value.

Your turn

Write the smallest three-digit number you can make using these digits.

●	1	8	7	__178__
a	7	9	8	____
b	2	9	1	____
c	4	1	0	____
d	3	9	7	____

SELF CHECK   Mark how you feel

| Got it! | Need help... | I don't get it |
| ☺ ☐ | 😐 ☐ | ☹ ☐ |

Check your answers
How many did you get correct?

PRACTICE

 1 What is the largest number you can make using these digits?

⬤ 3, 2, 4 __432__

a 1, 7, 9 _____   g 8, 1, 7 _____

b 8, 6, 4 _____   h 1, 0, 6 _____

c 4, 8, 9 _____   i 6, 3, 0 _____

d 7, 6, 8 _____   j 4, 1, 3 _____

e 1, 3, 2 _____   k 3, 4, 9 _____

f 5, 3, 9 _____   l 7, 4, 7 _____

 2 Color the larger three-digit number red and the smaller number green.

⬤ | 721 | 127 |

a | 542 | 245 | d | 975 | 579 |

b | 389 | 983 | e | 246 | 642 |

c | 406 | 640 | f | 831 | 138 |

3 Look at the three digits. Use them to make the largest and smallest three-digit numbers you can.

Digits	Largest Number	Smallest Number
③ ⑨ ①	931	139
a ⑦ ① ⑨		
b ⑤ ⓪ ④		
c ⑧ ⑥ ②		
d ④ ⑨ ③		
e ⑦ ⑧ ④		

PLACE VALUE TO 100

The place value is the value of a digit based on where it is in a number.

Example 1:   In the number **79**,
the place value of the **7** is **tens**
because the 7 is in the tens place,
and the place value of the **9** is **ones**
because the 9 is in the ones place.

Example 2:   **62** is a two-digit number that has
6 tens and **2 ones**.

Example 3:   **53** is a two-digit number that has
__ tens and __ ones.

> Look at the order of the place value— first tens, then ones.

Your turn

Circle the tens in blue and the ones in red in the numbers.

● ⑥⑧

29	93	43	72
	17	85	35
11	33	57	79
	94	48	20
62	81	99	40

SELF CHECK   Mark how you feel

Got it!	Need help...	I don't get it
☺ ☐	😐 ☐	😠 ☐

Check your answers
How many did you get correct?

PRACTICE

 1 Write the number for the place values shown.

⬤ 2 ones and 5 tens = __52__

   a 4 tens and 1 one = _____

   b 6 ones and 3 tens = _____

   c 7 ones and 8 tens = _____

   d 1 ten and 4 ones = _____

   e 7 tens and 5 ones = _____

   f 8 tens and 8 ones = _____

   g 9 ones and 3 tens = _____

   h 2 tens and 3 ones = _____

 2 Match the place-value cards to the numbers.

⬤
tens	ones
5	4

a
tens	ones
4	0

b
tens	ones
8	5

c
tens	ones
9	3

eighty-five	fifty-four	ninety-three	forty

3 Put a red circle around the numbers in the ones place.

⬤ 3⑨   **a** 68   **b** 90   **c** 44   **d** 17

 4 Cross out the numbers in the tens place.

⬤ ~~1~~6   **a** 49   **b** 87   **c** 40   **d** 98

 5 What is the place value of the 3 in these numbers?

⬤ 32 ___tens___

   a 43 _____

   b 23 _____

   c 13 _____

   d 37 _____

   e 32 _____

   f 73 _____

   g 93 _____

   h 38 _____

   i 53 _____

NUMBER EXPANDERS FOR THREE-DIGIT NUMBERS

Here is a number expander for the number 378:

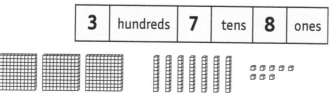

SCAN to watch video

If we fold the number expander to make 378 using only tens and ones, we have:

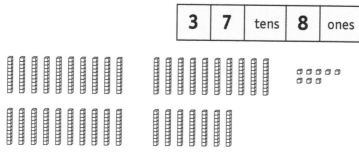

Look at the order of the place value—first hundreds, then tens, then ones.

If we fold the number expander again and make 378 using only ones, we have:

| 3 | 7 | 8 | ones |

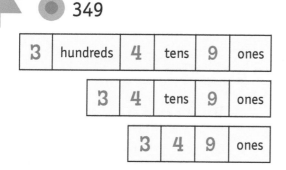

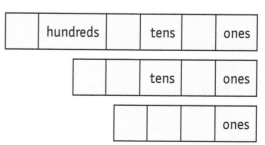

Complete the number expander.

349

| 3 | hundreds | 4 | tens | 9 | ones |

| | | 3 | 4 | tens | 9 | ones |

| | | | 3 | 4 | 9 | ones |

a 135

| | hundreds | | tens | | ones |

| | | | tens | | ones |

| | | | | | ones |

PRACTICE

 Fill in the number expanders.

243

2	hundreds	4	tens	3	ones

	2	4	tens	3	ones

		2	4	3	ones

a 342

	hundreds		tens		ones

			tens		ones

					ones

b 560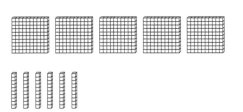

	hundreds		tens		ones

			tens		ones

					ones

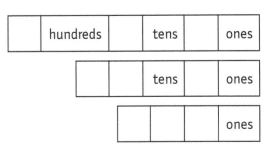

 Write the number shown on each number expander.

5	3	tens	4	ones

_534_

b
3	4	7	ones

_____

a
2	hundreds	4	tens	9	ones

_____

c
9	8	tens	1	ones

_____

 Fill in the numbers on each number expander.

329

3	hundreds	2	tens	9	ones

b 643

	hundreds		tens		ones

a 723

		tens		ones

c 178

			ones

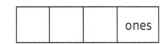

VALUES

The value of a number is how much it is worth.

Example 1:

623

The value of
the 6 is 600.

The value of
the 2 is 20.

The value of
the 3 is 3.

Example 2:

178

The value of
the 1 is _____.

The value of
the 7 is ___.

The value of
the 8 is __.

> When you put a number in a different place, it has a different value.

Even though 1 is the smallest number, it has the greatest value as it is in the hundreds place.

Your turn

In each number, circle in green the digit with the greatest value. Circle in red the digit with the least value.

⬤ (5)3(7)

777	416	909
140	102	849

738   625   186   236

SELF CHECK Mark how you feel

Got it! ☐   Need help... ☐   I don't get it ☐

Check your answers
How many did you get correct?

PRACTICE

 Write the numbers.

⬤ 3 hundreds, 6 tens, 3 ones = __363__

a 2 hundreds, 8 ones, 7 tens = _____

b 3 ones, 4 tens, 6 hundreds = _____

c 5 tens, 8 hundreds, 1 ones = _____

d 2 tens, 7 ones, 4 hundreds = _____

 Circle the digits with a value of 4. One is done for you.

32④   415   634   149   874

136   942   247   429

 Circle the digits with a value of 80. One is done for you.

7⑧1   478   810   382   318

803   128   483   818   581

 Circle the digits with a value of 500. One is done for you.

⑤23   257   125   599   525

459   501   653   577

545   582   605   205

 Write five numbers that fit the description.

⬤ 5 has a value of 50   __52__   __453__   __952__   __650__   __159__

a 7 has a value of 700   ____ ____ ____ ____ ____

b 4 has a value of 4   ____ ____ ____ ____ ____

c 3 has a value of 30   ____ ____ ____ ____ ____

GREATER THAN, LESS THAN, EQUAL TO

>	**=**	**<**
the symbol for greater than	the symbol for equal to	the symbol for less than

SCAN to watch video

Example 1: 425 | > | 125

Read it: 425 is greater than 125 ✓ Yes

425 is equal to 125 ✗ No

425 is less than 125 ✗ No

Which number does the pointy end point to? That helps you tell the difference between < and >.

Example 2: 223 | = | 223

Read it: 223 is greater than 223 ✗ No

223 is equal to 223 ✓ Yes

223 is less than 223 ✗ No

Example 3: 124 | | 632

Read it: 124 is greater than 632 _____

124 is equal to 632 _____

124 is less than 632 _____

Your turn

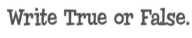

Write True or False.

● 724 = 124 __False__   c 241 = 241 _____

a 526 > 242 _____   d 736 > 523 _____

b 125 < 349 _____   e 825 > 852 _____

SELF CHECK   Mark how you feel

Got it!	Need help...	I don't get it
😀 ☐	😐 ☐	😠 ☐

Check your answers
How many did you get correct?

PRACTICE

 Use the symbols >, =, or < to complete.

235 $\boxed{>}$ 129

a 126 $\boxed{}$ 399   **c** 724 $\boxed{}$ 116   **e** 101 $\boxed{}$ 101

b 909 $\boxed{}$ 990   **d** 417 $\boxed{}$ 471   **f** 906 $\boxed{}$ 609

 Use the words $\boxed{\text{is greater than}}$, $\boxed{\text{is equal to}}$, or $\boxed{\text{is less than}}$ **to make these true.**

200 $\boxed{\text{is less than}}$ 300.

a 316 $\boxed{}$ 361.   **d** 210 $\boxed{}$ 201.

b 215 $\boxed{}$ 251.   **e** 883 $\boxed{}$ 883.

c 804 $\boxed{}$ 84.   **f** 680 $\boxed{}$ 680.

3 Circle the numbers described.

more than 14   12, (31), 10, (51)

a less than 22   1, 21, 25, 32

b more than 51   52, 53, 15, 7

c less than 69   44, 31, 96, 71

d less than 132   101, 123, 141, 158

e equal to 137   137, 173, 137, 731

f more than 625   526, 627, 597, 682

g equal to 451   154, 451, 541, 451

THREE-DIGIT NUMBERS

Example 1:

hundreds   tens   ones

729

seven hundred twenty-nine

When we write a three-digit number in words, first we look at the digit in the **hundreds place**. Here, it is a 7. So, the number starts with seven hundred.

Then, look at the **tens place**. The digit is a 2. So, the number would read seven hundred twenty.

Finally, look at the **ones place**. Here, it is a 9. So, the number is **seven hundred twenty-nine**.

> Use these words to help you.

one hundred	ten	one
two hundred	twenty	two
three hundred	thirty	three
four hundred	forty	four
five hundred	fifty	five
six hundred	sixty	six
seven hundred	seventy	seven
eight hundred	eighty	eight
nine hundred	ninety	nine

Example 2:

hundreds   tens   ones

634

This number is

_____

_____

Your turn

Write the numbers in words.

● 431 = <u>four hundred thirty-one</u>

a 248 = _____

b 952 = _____

PRACTICE

 Write these words as numbers.

● seven hundred twenty-three _723_

a two hundred forty-six _____

b eight hundred two _____

c four hundred fifty _____

d three hundred eighty _____

e nine hundred sixteen _____

f six hundred ninety-one _____

g seven hundred seventy-seven _____

h five hundred eight _____

 Write these numbers as words.

● 162 _one hundred sixty-two_

a 270 _____

b 313 _____

c 909 _____

d 821 _____

e 117 _____

f 999 _____

g 840 _____

h 511 _____

i 696 _____

ROUNDING TO THE NEAREST TEN

Rounding is useful when you need to estimate an answer.

Round-up numbers

9
8
7
6
5

Round-down numbers

4
3
2
1
0

When rounding to the nearest 10, follow these steps.

- Write the round up number above the tens column.
- Circle the number in the ones column.
- Decide if it is a round-up number or a round-down number.
- Round up or round down.

Example 1: Round 27 to the nearest 10.

Above the tens column, write the next number. ⟶ **3**
27

We are rounding down to 20 or rounding up to 30.

This number tells us whether we round up or down. **3**
2(7)

7 is a round-up number, so we round up to 30.

So, 27 rounded to the nearest 10 is **30**.

Example 2: Round 36 to the nearest 10.

36

Can you think of a time when you needed to estimate an amount?

Your turn

Round these numbers to the nearest 10.

6
53   **a** 31   **b** 76   **c** 92

50   ___   ___   ___

SELF CHECK   Mark how you feel

Got it!	Need help...	I don't get it
☺ ☐	😐 ☐	😠 ☐

Check your answers
How many did you get correct?

PRACTICE

 Round these numbers to the nearest 10.

4
● 3①
 30

c 24
____

f 29
____

a 56
____

d 99
____

g 68
____

b 72
____

e 43
____

h 55
____

2 **Round these three-digit numbers to the nearest 10.**

5
● 34②
 340

c 121
____

f 588
____

a 357
____

d 439
____

g 617
____

b 144
____

e 232
____

h 764
____

3 **Color the box that has the number correctly rounded to the nearest 10.**

● 493   **a** 605   **b** 971   **c** 844   **d** 358

490		600		970		840		350
500		610		980		850		360

FOUR-DIGIT NUMBERS

Writing four-digit numbers in words is similar to writing three-digit numbers in words.

Example 1: The number 2,483 has four digits.

The 2 has a value of two thousand.

The 4 has a value of four hundred.

The 8 has a value of eighty.

The 3 has a value of three.

2,483 written in words is
two thousand, four hundred eighty-three.

When a number is in a different place, it has a different value.

Example 2:

	Number	Th	H	T	O	Words
a	6,281	6	2	8	1	six thousand, two hundred eighty-one
b	4,032					four thousand thirty-two
c	5,903	5	9	0	3	

Your turn

Write the following numbers in words.

⬤ 4,136 <u>four thousand, one hundred thirty-six</u>

a 3,492 _____

b 6,057 _____

SELF CHECK Mark how you feel

Got it! ☺ ☐   Need help... 😐 ☐   I don't get it 😟 ☐ ·········▷ Check your answers
How many did you get correct?

PRACTICE

 Write these words as numbers.

- ● five thousand, three hundred forty-eight   _5,348_

- **a** six thousand, two hundred nineteen   _____

- **b** three thousand, seven hundred eleven   _____

- **c** eight thousand, two hundred sixteen   _____

- **d** nine thousand, five hundred thirty-seven   _____

 Write each number in words.

- ● 6,347 _six thousand, three hundred forty-seven_

- **a** 2,462 _____

- **b** 4,491 _____

- **c** 9,379 _____

 Write each set of numbers in ascending order (smallest to largest).

- ● 1,273; 2,495; 1,013; 3,498   _1,013_ , _1,273_ , _2,495_ , _3,498_

- **a** 2,468; 1,392; 8,743; 7,110   _____, _____, _____, _____

- **b** 3,740; 3,470; 2,498; 5,476   _____, _____, _____, _____

- **c** 8,219; 9,099; 9,990; 8,921   _____, _____, _____, _____

 Write each set of numbers in descending order (largest to smallest).

- ● 8,316; 2,481; 9,377; 3,313   _9,377_ , _8,316_ , _3,313_ , _2,481_

- **a** 1,249; 8,932; 2,495; 6,419   _____, _____, _____, _____

- **b** 7,116; 6,117; 1,716; 1,176   _____, _____, _____, _____

- **c** 8,211; 1,128; 8,121; 2,181   _____, _____, _____, _____

PLACE VALUE TO 1,000

The place value is the value of a digit based on where it is in a number.

In the number 658, the place value of the 6 is hundreds because it is in the hundreds place.

Example 1:

347 is a three-digit number that has 3 hundreds, 4 tens, and 7 ones.

Example 2:

739 is a three-digit number that has 7 hundreds, 3 tens, and 9 ones.

9 is the biggest number in 739, but it doesn't have the biggest value.

Example 3:

621 is a three-digit number that has __ hundreds, __ tens, and __ ones.

Your turn

Circle the hundreds in green, tens in blue, and ones in red.

7 1 3   3 0 2   9 3 1   2 4 1

229   850   170

436   519   352

SELF CHECK   Mark how you feel

Got it!	Need help...	I don't get it
☺ ☐	😐 ☐	☹ ☐

Check your answers

How many did you get correct?

PRACTICE

 Write the numbers.

⬤ 4 hundreds, 7 tens, 2 ones = <u>472</u>

a 1 hundred, 3 tens, 4 ones = _____

b 3 hundreds, 6 tens = _____

c 5 hundreds, 0 tens, 7 ones = _____

 Fill in the table.

Number	Hundreds	Tens	Ones
657	6	5	7
a 231			
b 859			
c 714			
d 902			
e 530			

 Cross out the numbers that have 4 tens.
Circle the numbers that have 2 hundreds.
Draw a rectangle around the numbers that have 7 ones.

777   740   817   417   293

251   349   540   298

 What is the place value of the 4 in these numbers: hundreds, tens, or ones?

⬤ 47   4   <u>tens</u>   **d** 342   4 _____

a 234   4 _____   **e** 14   4 _____

b 418   4 _____   **f** 243   4 _____

c 504   4 _____   **g** 493   4 _____

PLACE VALUE AND FOUR-DIGIT NUMBERS

The place value is the value of a digit based on where it is in a number.

Example 1:

The number 7,258 is a four-digit number that has a 7 in the thousands place, a 2 in the hundreds place, a 5 in the tens place, and an 8 in the ones place.

Example 2:

The number 1,369 is a four-digit number that has 1 thousand, 3 hundreds, 6 tens, and 9 ones.

Example 3:

4,273 is a four-digit number.

thousands —4,2(7)3— ones
hundreds tens

You can use different words to talk about the value of a number.

Thousands	Hundreds	Tens	Ones

Your turn

Circle the thousands purple, the hundreds green, the tens blue, and the ones red.

6,969   9,203   7,312   4,811

2,812   4,159   5,702   3,789   7,002

SELF CHECK Mark how you feel

Got it!   Need help...   I don't get it

Check your answers

How many did you get correct?

PRACTICE

 Fill in the table.

Number	Thousands	Hundreds	Tens	Ones
3,490	3	4	9	0
a 6,137				
b 8,451				
c 1,459				
d 5,458				
e 2,104				
f 7,002				

 Write the numbers.

- one thousand, 7 hundreds, 2 tens, 3 ones = __1,723__

- **a** 6 hundreds, 3 thousands, 1 tens, 7 ones = _____

- **b** 8 ones, 2 hundreds, 4 thousands, 5 tens = _____

- **c** 5 thousands, 6 hundreds, 3 tens, 8 ones = _____

- **d** 9 hundreds, 6 thousands, 4 tens, 1 ones = _____

3 Circle the following numbers in
   red that have 2 ones,
   blue that have 7 tens,
   green that have 9 hundreds, and
   purple that have 6 thousands.

4,963   3,878   2,573   4,812

5,471   8,242   6,735   5,945   6,423

1,422   3,913   1,070   3,470

EXPANDED FORM OF FOUR-DIGIT NUMBERS

SCAN to watch video

Four-digit numbers can be made with Base 10 blocks or an abacus and can be written in expanded form.

Example 1:

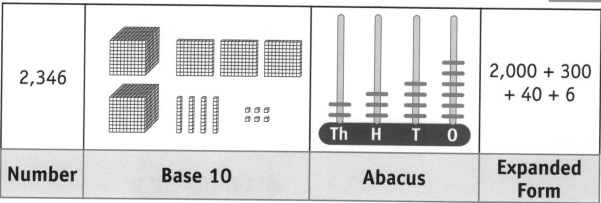

Number	Base 10	Abacus	Expanded Form
2,346			2,000 + 300 + 40 + 6

Example 2:

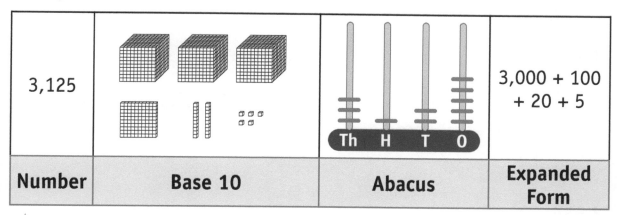

Number	Base 10	Abacus	Expanded Form
3,125			3,000 + 100 + 20 + 5

Your turn

1 Draw the Base 10 blocks you would use to make 1,432.

2 Write 1,432 in expanded form.

_____ + _____ + _____ + _____

SELF CHECK   Mark how you feel

Got it!	Need help...	I don't get it
☐	☐	☐

Check your answers
How many did you get correct?

PRACTICE

1 Fill in the table.

	Number	Base 10	Abacus	Expanded Form
	1,831		Th H T O	1,000 + 800 + 30 + 1
a	3,495		Th H T O	
b	4,321		Th H T O	
c	2,534		Th H T O	
d	7,103		Th H T O	

2 Write these numbers in expanded form.

● 2,937 = __2,000__ + __900__ + __30__ + __7__

a 4,716 = _____ + _____ + _____ + ____

b 9,219 = _____ + _____ + _____ + ____

c 3,203 = _____ + _____ + _____ + ____

d 6,180 = _____ + _____ + _____ + ____

e 5,271 = _____ + _____ + _____ + ____

f 1,394 = _____ + _____ + _____ + ____

g 7,536 = _____ + _____ + _____ + ____

h 8,625 = _____ + _____ + _____ + ____

3 Write the numbers in standard form.

● 5,000 + 300 + 20 + 1 = __5,321__

a 6,000 + 700 + 90 + 3 = _____

b 8,000 + 400 + 20 + 6 = _____

c 1,000 + 100 + 0 + 7 = _____

d 4,000 + 100 + 60 + 9 = _____

e 7,000 + 900 + 10 + 7 = _____

f 3,000 + 500 + 20 + 5 = _____

g 9,000 + 400 + 0 + 4 = _____

h 2,000 + 300 + 80 + 6 = _____

i 3,000 + 600 + 50 + 9 = _____

j 5,000 + 100 + 90 + 2 = _____

k 1,000 + 800 + 20 + 1 = _____

MODELING FOUR-DIGIT NUMBERS

A four-digit number can be made using Base 10 blocks.

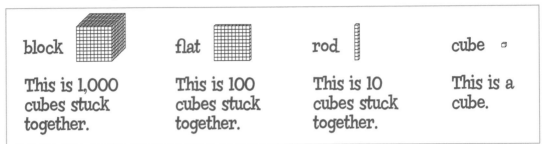

block	flat	rod	cube
This is 1,000 cubes stuck together.	This is 100 cubes stuck together.	This is 10 cubes stuck together.	This is a cube.

Example 1: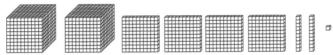

The four-digit number these Base 10 blocks make is 2,421.

Example 2: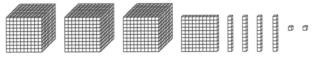

The four-digit number these Base 10 blocks make is 3,142.

How many rods would you stick together to make a flat?

Example 3:

The four-digit number these Base 10 blocks make is _____.

Your turn

What number does each set of Base 10 blocks make?

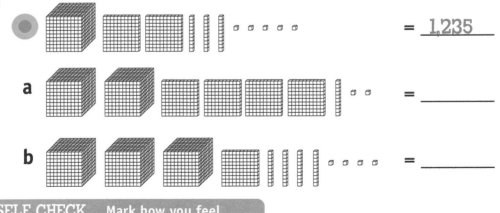

= 1,235

a _____ = _____

b _____ = _____

SELF CHECK Mark how you feel

Got it!	Need help...	I don't get it
☺ ☐	😐 ☐	☹ ☐

Check your answers
How many did you get correct?

PRACTICE

1 Color in the Base 10 blocks needed to make these numbers.

4,563

a 3,241

b 2,543

c 6,210

2 Show each number on the abacus.

2,153

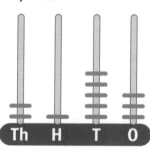

b 7,217

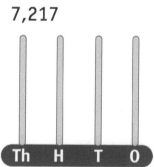

d 5,423

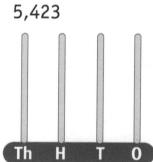

a 2,345

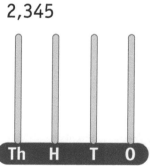

c 4,815

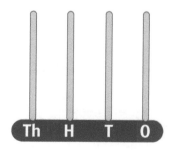

e 8,874

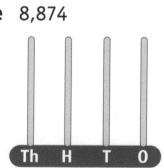

ROUNDING

Rounding to 10	Rounding to 100	Rounding to 1,000
1 Go to the tens column.	1 Go to the hundreds column.	1 Go to the thousands column.
2 Write the round-up number above the tens.	2 Write the round-up number above the hundreds.	2 Write the round-up number above the thousands.
3 Circle the number in the ones column.	3 Circle the number in the tens column.	3 Circle the number in the hundreds column.
4 Is it a round-up or round-down number?	4 Is it a round-up or round-down number?	4 Is it a round-up or round-down number?
5 Round your number.	5 Round your number.	5 Round your number.

Example 1: Round 26 to the nearest 10.

3
2(6) up 30

Example 2: Round 364 to the nearest 100.

4
3(6)4 up 400

Example 3: Round 4,236 to the nearest 1,000. _____

Round-down numbers					Round-up numbers				
0	1	2	3	4	5	6	7	8	9

Your turn

1 Round 43 to the nearest 10. _____

2 Round 124 to the nearest 10. _____

3 Round 256 to the nearest 100. _____

4 Round 1,327 to the nearest 100. _____

5 Round 2,468 to the nearest 1,000. _____

PRACTICE

1 Round these numbers to the nearest 10.

⬤ 2,35⑧ $\overset{6}{\curvearrowleft}$ up
    <u>2,360</u>

c 32

_____

f 276

_____

a 14

_____

d 481

_____

g 1,245

_____

b 25

_____

e 384

_____

h 3,279

_____

2 Round these numbers to the nearest 100.

⬤ 6,7⑥3 $\overset{8}{\curvearrowleft}$ up
    <u>6,800</u>

c 378

_____

f 4,095

_____

a 473

_____

d 9,891

_____

g 1,711

_____

b 524

_____

e 6,243

_____

h 9,691

_____

3 Round these numbers to the nearest 1,000.

⬤ 7,⑨71 $\overset{8}{\curvearrowleft}$ up
    <u>8,000</u>

b 5,845

_____

d 7,496

_____

a 3,243

_____

c 9,935

_____

e 1,821

_____

4 Round 5,473 to the nearest

a 10 _____

b 100 _____

c 1,000 _____

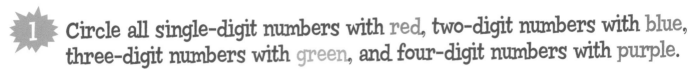

WHOLE NUMBERS REVIEW

1 Circle all single-digit numbers with red, two-digit numbers with blue, three-digit numbers with green, and four-digit numbers with purple.

47   1   123   5   38   711   4,151   8,258   3,206   4

2   457   13   506   26   69   1,289   4,007   747   6,328

2 What number comes before each of these numbers?

a 23 _____   **d** 426 _____   **g** 1,809 _____

b 37 _____   **e** 2,306 _____   **h** 4,728 _____

c 351 _____   **f** 4,120 _____

3 What number comes after each of these numbers?

a 16 _____   **d** 185 _____   **g** 1,836 _____

b 29 _____   **e** 290 _____   **h** 3,593 _____

c 213 _____   **f** 1,382 _____

4 Fill in the tables.

Number	Thousands	Hundreds	Tens	Ones
14	0	0	1	4
a 39				
b 85				
c 76				
d 204				
e 193				

	Number	Thousands	Hundreds	Tens	Ones
f	784				
g	830				
h	4,158				
i	6,007				
j	8,403				
k	9,093				

5 Write these numbers in expanded form.

a 15 = _____

b 22 = _____

c 181 = _____

d 256 = _____

e 490 = _____

f 2,593 = _____

g 3,849 = _____

h 6,452 = _____

6 Draw each number on the abacus.

a 51

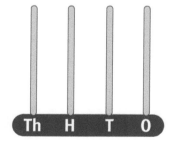

b 23

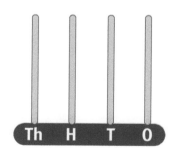

c 186

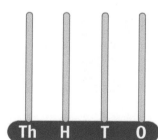

d 349

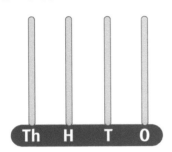

e 746

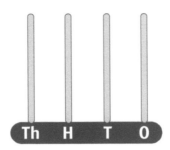

f 6,382

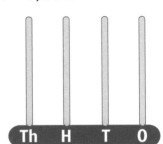

g 5,841

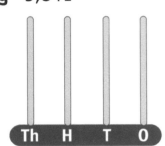

h 9,030

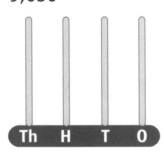

7 Color in the Base 10 blocks to show the numbers.

a 32

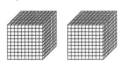

b 163

c 1,465

d 5,312

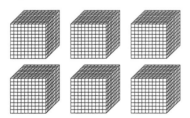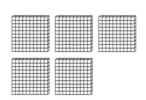

8 Fill in the missing spaces.

a   21, 23, 25, ____, ____, ____

b   47, 49, 51, ____, ____, ____

c   98, 96, 94, ____, ____, ____

d   72, 70, 68, ____, ____, ____

e   25, 30, 35, ____, ____, ____

f   90, 85, 80, ____, ____, ____

g   0, 5, 10, ____, ____, ____

h   70, 65, 60, ____, ____, ____

i   100, 90, 80, ____, ____, ____

j   20, 30, 40, ____, ____, ____

k   50, 40, 30, ____, ____, ____

l   70, 80, 90, ____, ____, ____

m   3, 13, 23, ____, ____, ____

n   54, 44, 34, ____, ____, ____

o   27, 37, 47, ____, ____, ____

p   99, 89, 79, ____, ____, ____

9 Write the rule for each pattern.

a   7, 12, 17, 22, 27   Rule _____

b   36, 39, 42, 45, 48   Rule _____

c   12, 22, 32, 42, 52   Rule _____

d   89, 84, 79, 74, 69   Rule _____

e   29, 27, 25, 23, 21   Rule _____

f   61, 51, 41, 31, 21   Rule _____

g   73, 70, 67, 64, 61   Rule _____

h   5, 9, 13, 17, 21   Rule _____

REVIEW

 10 Write these numbers in ascending order.

 a 126; 24; 315; 82; 463 _____

 b 37; 84; 16; 9; 125 _____

 c 347; 124; 65; 1,342; 91 _____

 d 1,311; 1,113; 3,111; 1,131; 1,011 _____

 11 Write these numbers in descending order.

 a 7; 243; 64; 911; 1,742 _____

 b 64; 157; 9; 1,359; 711 _____

 c 3,313; 246; 9,501; 89; 969 _____

 d 2,423; 2,234; 4,232; 3,422; 2,243 _____

12 Make the smallest and largest numbers from the digits shown.

	Digits	Largest	Smallest
a	543		
b	784		
c	549		
d	219		
e	373		
f	494		

 13 Write the numbers shown by these place values.

 a 6 thousands, 4 hundreds, 3 tens, 8 ones = _____

 b 8 hundreds, 5 thousands, 2 tens, 6 ones = _____

 c 7 ones, 4 hundreds, 1 tens, 9 thousands = _____

d 3 hundreds, 3 ones, 2 tens = _____

e 2 tens, 4 ones = _____

f 4 tens, 6 ones, 2 hundreds = _____

g 6 ones = _____

h 4 ones, 2 tens, 4 hundreds = _____

14 Put a blue X on the numbers that have 3 tens.
Put a green X on the numbers that have 4 hundreds.
Put a purple X on the numbers that have 2 thousands.
Put a red X on the numbers that have 8 ones.

4,235   58   630   3,421   4,444   37   2,349   258   8,936

28   415   3,348   333   479   8   2,929   2,157

15 Fill in the number expanders.

a 347

	hundreds		tens		ones

b 215

		tens		ones

c 873

			ones

d 378

	hundreds		tens		ones

		tens		ones

			ones

16 What is the value of the 3 in these numbers?

a 3,429 _____

b 136 _____

c 53 _____

d 327 _____

e 63 _____

f 3 _____

17 What is the value of the 5 in these numbers?

a 5 _____

b 75 _____

c 125 _____

d 514 _____

e 152 _____

f 5,127 _____

18 Write *True* or *False*.

a 425 < 125 _____

b 136 = 136 _____

c 743 > 211 _____

d 814 < 1,242 _____

e 1,006 = 6,001 _____

f 29 < 92 _____

g 3,210 > 3,201 _____

h 767 < 843 _____

i 364 < 563 _____

j 912 < 345 _____

k 1,435 > 1,263 _____

l 747 > 4,931 _____

19 Write >, =, or < to complete.

a 127 ___ 499

b 660 ___ 606

c 726 ___ 611

d 709 ___ 907

e 660 ___ 660

f 210 ___ 102

g 886 ___ 886

h 973 ___ 369

i 513 ___ 691

20 Round to the nearest 10.

a 8 _____

b 12 _____

c 18 _____

d 123 _____

e 498 _____

f 531 _____

g 626 _____

h 1,432 _____

i 7,491 _____

j 8,434 _____

21 Round to the nearest 100.

a 329 _____

b 415 _____

c 642 _____

d 5,493 _____

e 6,371 _____

f 4,591 _____

22 Round to the nearest 1,000.

a 1,436 _____

b 2,899 _____

c 7,044 _____

d 8,606 _____

e 9,377 _____

f 9,524 _____

23 Complete the table.

	Number	Round to nearest 10	Round to nearest 100	Round to nearest 1,000
a	7,493			
b	5,812			
c	3,567			

24 Write these numbers in words.

a 17 _____

b 28 _____

c 159 _____

d 306 _____

e 5,342_____

_____

f 8,909_____

_____

ADDING NUMBERS TO TEN

We have 10 fingers.
Use your fingers to help you
add and subtract to 10.

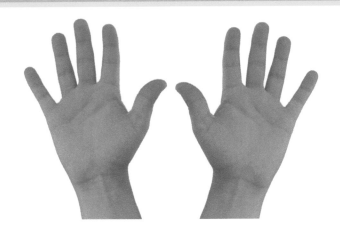

Example 1:

5 + ___ = 10

If I put 5 of my 10 fingers down,
there are 5 fingers left up, so 5 + 5 = 10.

Example 2:

7 + ___ = 10

If I put ___ of my 10 fingers down,
there are ___ fingers left up, so 7 + ___ = 10.

> When you use
> your fingers to
> see the numbers,
> it helps you
> remember how
> to make 10.

Your turn

1 Use your fingers to do these addition problems.

a   3 + ___ = 10   c   1 + ___ = 10

b   4 + ___ = 10   d   8 + ___ = 10

2 Look for numbers that add to 10, and circle them.
Then, add the last number to the circled number.

● 3 + ④ + ⑥ = 4 + 6 + 3   a   7 + 1 + 3 = _____

= 10 + 3   = _____

= 13   = ___

SELF CHECK   Mark how you feel

Got it!	Need help...	I don't get it

Check your answers
How many did
you get correct?

PRACTICE

1 Look for numbers that add to 10, and circle them. Then, add the last number to the circled number.

⬤ (7) + 4 + (3) = (7 + 3) + 4 _____

= 10 + 4 _____

= 14 ___

a 9 + 1 + 2 = _____

= _____

= ___

b 8 + 5 + 2 = _____

= _____

= ___

c 7 + 7 + 3 = _____

= _____

= ___

d 4 + 9 + 6 = _____

= _____

= ___

e 7 + 3 + 5 = _____

= _____

= ___

f 8 + 8 + 2 = _____

= _____

= ___

g 1 + 8 + 9 = _____

= _____

= ___

h 4 + 6 + 7 = _____

= _____

= ___

i 6 + 5 + 4 = _____

= _____

= ___

j 5 + 5 + 6 = _____

= _____

= ___

k 7 + 6 + 3 = _____

= _____

= ___

ADDING NUMBERS TO TWENTY

A number line can be used to solve addition problems.

Example 1:

Solve: 5 + ___ = 20

15 jumps to get to 20

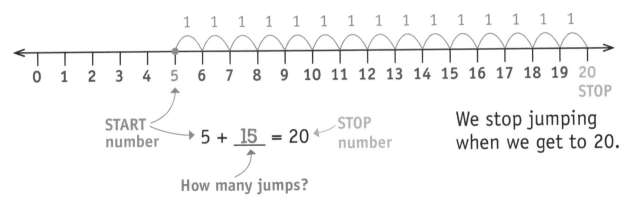

20
STOP

START
number → 5 + _15_ = 20 ← STOP
number

How many jumps?

We stop jumping when we get to 20.

Example 2:

Solve: 13 + ___ = 20

___ jumps to get to 20

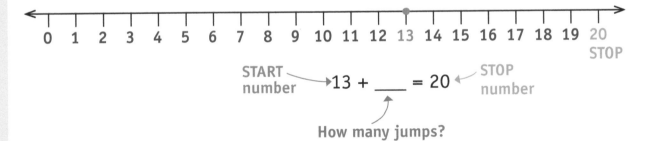

20
STOP

START
number → 13 + ___ = 20 ← STOP
number

How many jumps?

Your turn

Solve: 6 + ___ = 20

What is the start number?

0 1 2 3 4 5 6 7 8 9 10 11 12 13 14 15 16 17 18 19 20

SELF CHECK   Mark how you feel

Got it!	Need help...	I don't get it

Check your answers
How many did you get correct?

PRACTICE

1 Complete these addition problems.

a 14 + ___ = 20

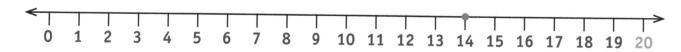

b 3 + ___ = 20

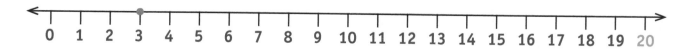

c 2 + ___ = 20

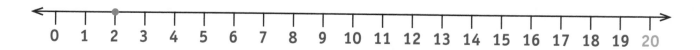

2 Write the missing numbers.

a 15 + ___ = 20

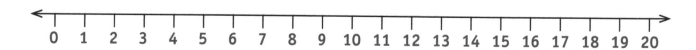

b 19 + ___ = 20

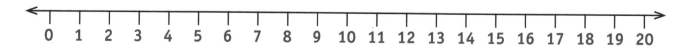

c 9 + ___ = 20

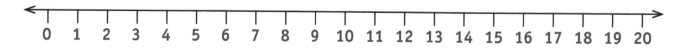

d 8 + ___ = 20

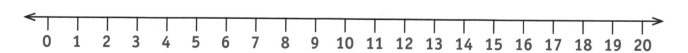

ADDITION AND SUBTRACTION

SCAN to watch video

The symbol + is used when adding.
The symbol − is used when subtracting (taking away).

Addition and subtraction are OPPOSITE operations.

Example 1:

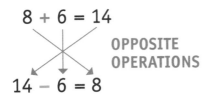

$8 + 6 = 14$

OPPOSITE OPERATIONS

$14 - 6 = 8$

Example 3:

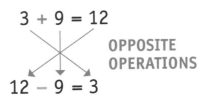

$3 + 9 = 12$

OPPOSITE OPERATIONS

$12 - 9 = 3$

Example 2:

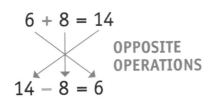

$6 + 8 = 14$

OPPOSITE OPERATIONS

$14 - 8 = 6$

Example 4:

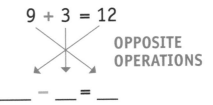

$9 + 3 = 12$

OPPOSITE OPERATIONS

___ − __ = __

Your turn

Fill in the missing numbers.

a $7 + 4 = 11$

$11 - \underline{} = 7$

$4 + 7 = \underline{}$

$11 - \underline{} = 4$

b $8 + 9 = 17$

$17 - \underline{} = 8$

$9 + \underline{} = 17$

$\underline{} - 8 = 9$

c $5 + 7 = 12$

$12 - \underline{} = 5$

$7 + \underline{} = 12$

$12 - \underline{} = 7$

d $7 + 13 = 20$

$20 - \underline{} = 7$

$13 + \underline{} = 20$

$20 - 7 = \underline{}$

Can you see the patterns in each set?

SELF CHECK   Mark how you feel

Got it!

Need help...

I don't get it

Check your answers
How many did you get correct?

PRACTICE

1 Complete the following.

● 15 + 5 = 20

    20 − _5_ = 15

c 20 + 0 = 20

    20 − ____ = 20

a 16 + 4 = 20

    20 − ____ = 16

d 10 + 10 = 20

    20 − ____ = 10

b 11 + 9 = 20

    20 − ____ = 11

e 8 + 12 = 20

    20 − ____ = 8

2 Fill in the missing numbers.

● 15 + 5 = 20

    20 − _5_ = 15

    5 + 15 = _20_

    _20_ − 15 = 5

c 14 + 2 = 16

    ____ − 2 = 14

    2 + ____ = 16

    ____ − 14 = 2

f 13 + 5 = 18

    ____ − ____ = ____

    ____ + ____ = ____

    ____ − ____ = ____

a 1 + 19 = 20

    ____ − 19 = 1

    19 + ____ = 20

    20 − 1 = ____

d 8 + 5 = 13

    13 − ____ = 8

    ____ + 8 = 13

    13 − ____ = 5

g 11 + 5 = 16

    ____ − ____ = ____

    ____ + ____ = ____

    ____ − ____ = ____

b 12 + 8 = 20

    20 − ____ = 12

    ____ + 12 = 20

    20 − ____ = 8

e 7 + 4 = 11

    ____ − 4 = 7

    4 + ____ = 11

    11 − ____ = 4

h 17 + 2 = 19

    ____ − ____ = ____

    ____ + ____ = ____

    ____ − ____ = ____

JUMP STRATEGY TO SOLVE ADDITION

The jump strategy uses a number line to find the answers to addition questions.

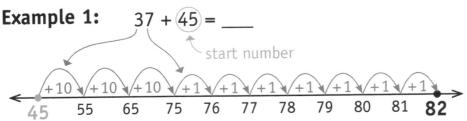

Example 1:   37 + (45) = ___

start number

+10 +10 +10 +1 +1 +1 +1 +1 +1 +1

45   55   65   75   76   77   78   79   80   81   **82**

37

3 big "tens" jumps ⤻ ⤸ 7 little "ones" jumps

So, 37 + 45 = 82

STEPS

| 1 First, write the bigger number on the number line. | 2 Then, find the number of big "tens" jumps, and draw them on the number line. | 3 Next, find the number of little "ones" jumps, and draw them on the number line. | 4 Count forward from the first number you wrote on the number line to find the answer. |

Example 2:   (63) + 24 = ___

start number

+10 +10

63   73   83

24

__ big "tens" jumps ⤻ ⤸ __ little "ones" jumps

So, 63 + 24 = ____

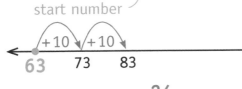

How many little "ones" jumps?

Your turn

Use the number line to solve 58 + 23.

<————————————•————————————————————>

SELF CHECK   Mark how you feel

| Got it! | Need help... | I don't get it |

Check your answers
How many did you get correct?

© Shell Education

PRACTICE

1 Use the number lines to add these numbers.

a 71 + 15 = _____

b 27 + 38 = _____

c 53 + 26 = _____

d 24 + 35 = _____

e 33 + 52 = _____

f 71 + 24 = _____

g 43 + 27 = _____

h 94 + 18 = _____

JUMP STRATEGY WITH LARGER NUMBERS

When adding big numbers, we can use the jump method to find the answer.

Example 1: What is 823 + 56?

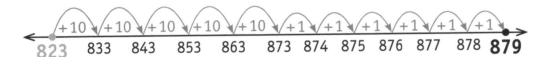

823 + 56 — 6 little "ones" jumps
↑ 5 big "tens" jumps
start number

+10 +10 +10 +10 +10 +1 +1 +1 +1 +1 +1
823   833   843   853   863   873 874 875 876 877 878 **879**

So, 823 + 56 = 879

Example 2: What is 724 + 32?

724 + 32
↑
start number

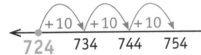

+10 +10 +10
724   734   744   754

So, 724 + 32 = _____

How many little "ones" jumps?

Your turn

What is 442 + 37?

PRACTICE

1 Use the number lines to add these numbers.

● 523 + 41 = __564__

523   533   543   553   563   **564**
+10   +10   +10   +10   +1

a 714 + 25 = _____

b 327 + 43 = _____

c 421 + 56 = _____

d 234 + 73 = _____

e 843 + 57 = _____

f 647 + 22 = _____

g 934 + 31 = _____

h 133 + 44 = _____

SPLIT STRATEGY TO SOLVE THE ADDITION OF TWO-DIGIT NUMBERS

When using the split strategy, we "split" the numbers into tens and ones.

5 | 1
tens : one

3 | 2
tens : ones

4 | 7
tens : ones

Example 1: Let's solve 54 + 31.

5 tens = 50   3 tens = 30

5 | 4   +   3 | 1
tens : ones   tens : one

→ 50 + 30 = 80 and 4 + 1 = 5

80 + 5

85

Example 2: Solve 32 + 25.

32 + 25 → ____ + ____ = ____ and __ + __ = __

____ + __

____

What is 3 tens equal to?

Your turn

Solve 63 + 26 using the split strategy.

63 + 26 → ____ + ____ = ____ and __ + __ = __

____ + __

____

SELF CHECK   Mark how you feel

Got it! ☐   Need help... ☐   I don't get it ☐

Check your answers
How many did you get correct?

PRACTICE

1 Answer these questions using the split strategy.

● 32 + 21 → __30__ + __20__ = __50__ and _2_ + _1_ = _3_

__50__ + _3_

__53__

a 28 + 21 → ____ + ____ = ____ and __ + __ = __

____ + __

____

b 71 + 14 → ____ + ____ = ____ and __ + __ = __

____ + __

____

c 55 + 13 → ____ + ____ = ____ and __ + __ = __

____ + __

____

d 51 + 24 → ____ + ____ = ____ and __ + __ = __

____ + __

____

e 36 + 12 → ____ + ____ = ____ and __ + __ = __

____ + __

____

f 23 + 52 → ____ + ____ = ____ and __ + __ = __

____ + __

____

SPLIT STRATEGY TO SOLVE THE ADDITION OF LARGER NUMBERS

Even when adding big numbers, we can use the split strategy to work out the answers.

SCAN to watch video

Example 1: Solve 821 + 54.

821 + 54 = 800 and 20 + 50 = 70 and 1 + 4 = 5

800 + 70 + 5

875

So, 821 + 54 = 875

Example 2: Solve 435 + 51.

435 + 51 → __00 and __0 + __0 = _____ and 5 + 1 = __

_____ + _____ + __

_____

So, 435 + 51 = _____

What numbers are in the tens place?

Your turn

Add these numbers using the split strategy.

a 724 + 53 → __00 and __0 + __0 = _____ and 4 + 3 = __

_____ + _____ + __

_____

b 472 + 26 → __00 and __0 + __0 = _____ and 2 + 6 = __

_____ + _____ + __

_____

SELF CHECK   Mark how you feel

Got it! ☐   Need help... ☐   I don't get it ☐

Check your answers

How many did you get correct?

PRACTICE

1 Add these numbers using the split strategy.

642 + 31 → __600__ and __40__ + __30__ = __70__ and __2__ + __1__ = __3__

__600__ + __70__ + __3__

__673__

a 853 + 14 → _____ and _____ + _____ = _____ and __ + __ = __

= _____ + _____ + __

= _____

b 723 + 56 → _____ and _____ + _____ = _____ and __ + __ = __

_____ + _____ + __

_____

c 642 + 51 → _____ and _____ + _____ = _____ and __ + __ = __

_____ + _____ + __

_____

d 235 + 44 → _____ and _____ + _____ = _____ and __ + __ = __

_____ + _____ + __

_____

e 542 + 27 → _____ and _____ + _____ = _____ and __ + __ = __

_____ + _____ + __

_____

f 143 + 32 → _____ and _____ + _____ = _____ and __ + __ = __

_____ + _____ + __

_____

ADDITION REVIEW

 1 Make 10.

    a 7 + _____ = 10   **d** _____ + 3 = 10

    b 2 + _____ = 10   **e** _____ + 8 = 10

    c 6 + _____ = 10   **f** _____ + 5 = 10

 2 Circle the sums of 10, and add the numbers.

    a 3 + 5 + 7   **d** 4 + 1 + 6

       = _____   = _____

       = _____   = _____

    b 7 + 9 + 1   **e** 9 + 0 + 1

       = _____   = _____

       = _____   = _____

    c 8 + 2 + 4   **f** 8 + 3 + 7

       = _____   = _____

       = _____   = _____

 3 Use the number lines to solve the addition problems.

    a 6 + ____ = 20

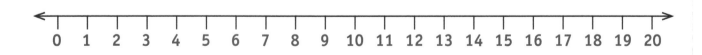

b 13 + ___ = 20

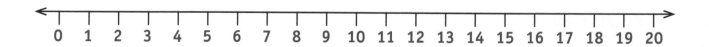

c ___ + 17 = 22

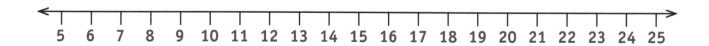

d ___ + 19 = 35

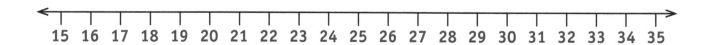

4 Fill in the missing numbers.

a 9 + 6 = _____

    15 – _____ = 9

    6 + 9 = _____

    15 – _____ = 6

b 12 + 8 = _____

    20 – _____ = 8

    8 + _____ = 20

    _____ – 8 = 12

c 15 + _____ = 20

    _____ – 5 = 15

    5 + _____ = 20

    _____ – 15 = 5

REVIEW

5 Use the number lines and the jump strategy to add the numbers.

a 38 + 49 = _____

b 83 + 25 = _____

c 57 + 42 = _____

d 32 + 44 = _____

e 424 + 53 = _____

f 235 + 21 = _____

g 762 + 58 = _____

h 142 + 12 = _____

i 510 + 23 = _____

j 842 + 20 = _____

6 Use the split strategy to add these numbers.

a 67 + 42 → __0 + __0 and __ + __

___0 + __

_____

b 58 + 31 → ____ + ____ and __ + __

____ + __

____

c 17 + 22 → ____ + ____ and __ + __

____ + __

____

d 43 + 35 → ____ + ____ and __ + __

= ____ + __

= ____

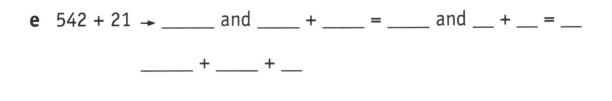

e 542 + 21 → _____ and ____ + ____ = ____ and __ + __ = __

____ + ____ + __

____

f 836 + 23 → _____ and ____ + ____ = ____ and __ + __ = __

____ + ____ + __

____

g 413 + 61 → _____ and ____ + ____ = ____ and __ + __ = __

____ + ____ + __

____

h 273 + 14 → _____ and ____ + ____ = ____ and __ + __ = __

____ + ____ + __

____

USING A NUMBER LINE FOR SUBTRACTION

The following number line shows how you can solve these subtraction problems.

Example 1: Solve 15 – 6.

START number → 15 – 6 = 9 ← Where do you finish?

Jump back

We move backward because we are subtracting.

$$-1 \quad -1 \quad -1 \quad -1 \quad -1 \quad -1$$

9 10 11 12 13 14 15

Example 2: Solve 13 – 4.

START number → 13 – 4 = ___ ← Where do you finish?

Jump back

13

Backward is from right to left.

Your turn

Use the number lines to solve these problems.

a 12 – 3 = ___   **b** 16 – 7 = ___

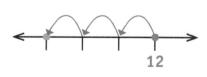

12

16

PRACTICE

    ● 14 – 6 = __8__

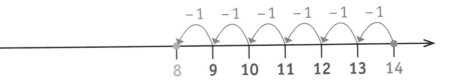

    a 15 – 7 = ___

    b 13 – 2 = ___

    c 16 – 12 = ___

    d 19 – 13 = ___

    e 12 – 8 = ___

    f 25 – 7 = ___

    g 32 – 6 = ___

SUBTRACTING NUMBERS FROM TEN

We have 10 fingers on our hands.

Your hands are helpful here!

Example 1:

10 – 5 = 5

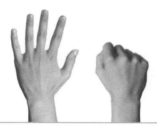

If I have 10 fingers and I put down 5, I have 5 fingers left.

Example 2:

10 – 3 = 7

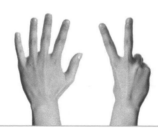

If I have 10 fingers and I put down 3, I have 7 fingers left.

Example 3:

10 – 7 = ___

If I have 10 fingers and I put down ___, I have ___ fingers left.

Your turn

Use your fingers to subtract these numbers.

a 10 – 2 = ___   d 10 – 9 = ___

b 10 – 1 = ___   e 10 – 6 = ___

c 10 – 4 = ___   f 10 – 0 = ___

SELF CHECK   Mark how you feel

Got it!	Need help...	I don't get it
☐	☐	☐

Check your answers
How many did you get correct?

PRACTICE

1 Use the number lines to solve the problems.

10 – 3 = _7_

a 10 – 6 = ___

b 10 – 9 = ___

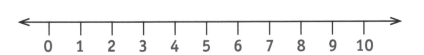

c 10 – 0 = ___

d 10 – 5 = ___

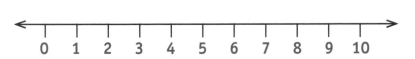

2 Match each picture with the correct number sentence.

10 – 5

b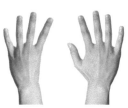

10 – 4

a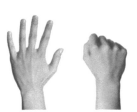

10 – 2

c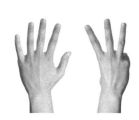

10 – 1

SUBTRACTING NUMBERS FROM TWENTY USING A NUMBER LINE

Subtraction problems can be solved using a number line.

Example 1: Solve 20 – 5.

20 – 5 = <u>15</u>

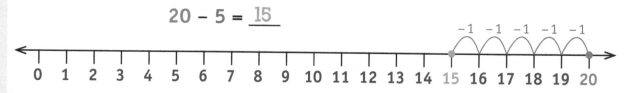

Example 2: Solve 20 – 13.

20 – 13 = ___

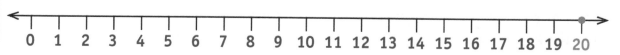

Subtract means jump backward.

Your turn

Solve each problem using the number line.

a 20 – 3 = ___

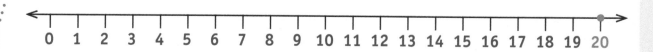

b 20 – 11 = ___

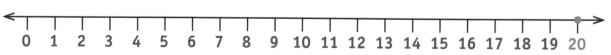

PRACTICE

1 Use the number lines to solve the subtraction problems.

⬤ 20 – 16 = __4__

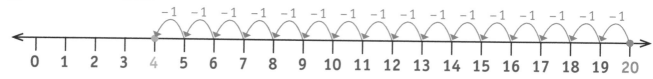

a 20 – 9 = ___

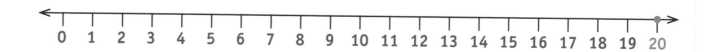

b 20 – 14 = ___

c 20 – 8 = ___

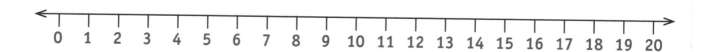

d 20 – 10 = ___

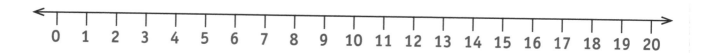

e 20 – 1 = ___

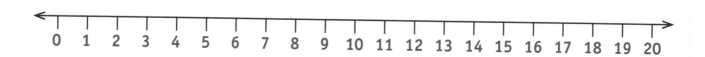

JUMP STRATEGY WITH TWO-DIGIT NUMBERS

A number line and the jump strategy can be used to solve subtraction problems.

Example 1: Solve 47 − 35 using the jump strategy.

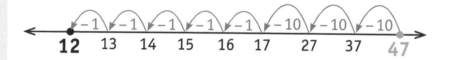

47 − 35 = ___

3 big "tens" jumps ⟋ ⟍ 5 little "ones" jumps

$$\overset{-1}{\frown}\ \overset{-1}{\frown}\ \overset{-1}{\frown}\ \overset{-1}{\frown}\ \overset{-1}{\frown}\ \overset{-10}{\frown}\ \overset{-10}{\frown}\ \overset{-10}{\frown}$$

12 13 14 15 16 17 27 37 47

So, 47 − 35 = 12

We move backward on the number line because we are subtracting.

STEPS

| 1 Write the bigger number on the number line. | 2 How many big "tens" jumps do you need? | 3 How many little "ones" jumps do you need? | 4 Count the jumps to find your answer. |

Example 2: Solve 68 − 42 using the jump strategy.

68 − 42 = ___

68

So, 68 − 42 = ___

Your turn

Use this number line to work out 73 − 15.

73

So, 73 − 15 = ___

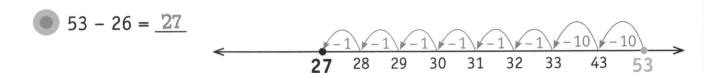

1 Use the number lines to subtract these numbers.

● 53 − 26 = <u>27</u>

27 28 29 30 31 32 33 43 53

a 45 − 24 = ___

b 52 − 43 = ___

c 71 − 54 = ___

d 82 − 31 = ___

e 42 − 25 = ___

f 63 − 42 = ___

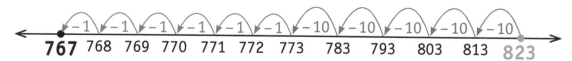

JUMP STRATEGY WITH LARGER NUMBERS

We can use the jump strategy to subtract big numbers.

Example 1: Solve 823 – 56 using the jump strategy.

823 – 56 = _____

767 768 769 770 771 772 773   783   793   803   813   823

So, 823 – 56 = 767

Example 2: Solve 724 – 32 using the jump strategy.

724 – 32 = _____

724

So, 724 – 32 = _____

Your turn

Subtract these numbers using the jump strategy.

a 523 – 41 = ___

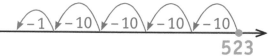

523

b 714 – 29 = ___

714

PRACTICE

1 Subtract these numbers using the jump strategy and the number lines.

● 327 – 43 = ___284___

284 285 286 287 297 307 317 327

a 524 – 33 = _____

b 647 – 28 = _____

c 421 – 56 = _____

d 284 – 41 = _____

e 934 – 42 = _____

f 873 – 67 = _____

SUBTRACTION USING THE SPLIT STRATEGY

When using the split strategy, we "split" the numbers into "tens" and "ones."

5 7 – **3 4**
tens ones   tens ones

The 5 is worth 50 because it is in the tens column.

The 7 is worth 7 because it is in the ones column.

The 3 is worth 30 because it is in the tens column.

The 4 is worth 4 because it is in the ones column.

Example 1: Solve 57 – 34.

57 – 34 → 50 – 30 = 20 and 7 – 4 = 3

20 + 3

23

We change the sign to +.

Example 2: Solve 74 – 23.

74 – 23 → __0 – __0 = ___ and __ – __ = __

___ + __

___

Your turn

Solve using the split strategy.

74 – 33 → __0 – __0 = ____ and __ – __ = __

= ____ + __

= ____

SELF CHECK Mark how you feel

Got it! □   Need help... □   I don't get it □

Check your answers
How many did you get correct?

PRACTICE

 Fill in the missing numbers.

● 83 – 22 → __80__ – __20__ = __60__ and _3_ – _2_ = _1_

        __60__ + _1_

        __61__

a   72 – 31 → ____ – ____ = ____ and __ – __ = __

            ____ + __

            ____

b   58 – 24 → ____ – ____ = ____ and __ – __ = __

            ____ + __

            ____

c   64 – 41 → ____ – ____ = ____ and __ – __ = __

            ____ + __

            ____

d   93 – 52 → ____ – ____ = ____ and __ – __ = __

            ____ + __

            ____

e   43 – 22 → ____ – ____ = ____ and __ – __ = __

            ____ + __

            ____

f   68 – 27 → ____ – ____ = ____ and __ – __ = __

            ____ + __

            ____

SUBTRACTION USING THE SPLIT STRATEGY WITH LARGER NUMBERS

Even when subtracting big numbers, we can use the split strategy.

Example 1: Solve 854 – 21.

854 – 21 = 800 and 50 – 20 = 30 and 4 – 1 = 3

            = 800 + 30 + 3

            = 833

We change the signs to +.

Example 2: Solve 735 – 23.

735 – 23 → 700 and __0 – __0 = __0 and __ – __ = __

            = __00 + __0 + __

            = ____

Your turn

Subtract these numbers using the split strategy.

527 – 13 → <u>500</u> and <u>20</u> – <u>10</u> = <u>10</u> and <u>7</u> – <u>3</u> = <u>4</u>

            = <u>500</u> + <u>10</u> + <u>4</u>

            = <u>514</u>

a 684 – 53 → _____ and ____ – ____ = ____ and __ – __ = __

            = ____ + ____ + __

            = ____

SELF CHECK Mark how you feel

Got it!	Need help...	I don't get it
☐	☐	☐

Check your answers

How many did you get correct?

PRACTICE

 1 Subtract these numbers using the split strategy.

○ 482 – 71 → <u>400</u> and <u>80</u> – <u>70</u> = <u>10</u> and <u>2</u> – <u>1</u> = <u>1</u>

<u>400</u> + <u>10</u> + <u>1</u>

<u>411</u>

a 859 – 38 → _____ and ____ – ____ = ____ and __ – __ = __

_____ + ____ + __

_____

b 586 – 43 → _____ and ____ – ____ = ____ and __ – __ = __

_____ + ____ + __

_____

c 747 – 35 → _____ and ____ – ____ = ____ and __ – __ = __

_____ + ____ + __

_____

d 572 – 51 → _____ and ____ – ____ = ____ and __ – __ = __

_____ + ____ + __

_____

e 732 – 11 → _____ and ____ – ____ = ____ and __ – __ = __

_____ + ____ + __

_____

f 457 – 26 → _____ and ____ – ____ = ____ and __ – __ = __

_____ + ____ + __

_____

1 Subtract these numbers using the number lines.

a 15 – 8 = ___

b 14 – 3 = ___

c 27 – 5 = ___

d 39 – 3 = ___

2 Fill in the missing numbers.

a 10 – ___ = 3

b 10 – ___ = 6

c ___ – 1 = 9

d 20 – 13 = ___

e 20 – ___ = 2

f 20 – ___ = 7

REVIEW

3 Use the jump strategy and the number lines to solve these problems.

a 68 – 47 = _____

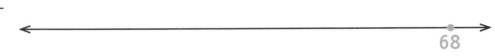
68

b 84 – 21 = _____

84

c 76 – 32 = _____

76

d 856 – 24 = _____

856

e 925 – 13 = _____

925

f 737 – 25 = _____

737

4 Subtract these numbers using the split strategy.

a 58 – 35 → _____ – _____ = _____ and __ – __ = __

_____ + __

_____

b 67 – 42 → ____ – ____ = ____ and __ – __ = __

               ____ + __

               ____

c 83 – 22 → ____ – ____ = ____ and __ – __ = __

               ____ + __

               ____

d 57 – 36 → ____ – ____ = ____ and __ – __ = __

               ____ + __

               ____

e 937 – 25 → _____ and ____ – ____ = ____ and __ – __ = __

               ____ + ____ + __

               ____

f 638 – 27 → _____ and ____ – ____ = ____ and __ – __ = __

               ____ + ____ + __

               ____

g 762 – 41 → _____ and ____ – ____ = ____ and __ – __ = __

               ____ + ____ + __

               ____

h 478 – 65 → _____ and ____ – ____ = ____ and __ – __ = __

               ____ + ____ + __

               _____

GROUPS AND ROWS

  Objects near each other are in groups.
There are four faces in this group.

When objects are in a line, they are in rows.
There are three stars in this row.

Example 1: 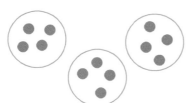 There are 3 groups of 4.

Example 2: There are 2 rows of 4.

Example 3:   There are __ groups of __.

What's the difference between a "group" and a "row"?

Your turn

1 Fill in the missing numbers.

2 rows of 5

a

__ rows of __

2 Fill in the missing numbers.

3 groups of 2

a

__ groups of __

SELF CHECK   Mark how you feel

Got it!	Need help...	I don't get it
☐	😐 ☐	😠 ☐

Check your answers
How many did you get correct?

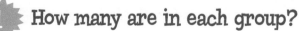

PRACTICE

1 How many are in each group?

_4_ in each group

a
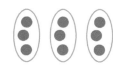

___ in each group

b

___ in each group

2 How many are in each row?

_6_ in each row

a

___ in each row

b

___ in each row

3 Draw extra objects to make these groups equal.

3 groups of 4

b 4 groups of 5

a 2 groups of 3

c 1 group of 5

4 Draw extra objects to make these rows equal.

3 rows of 2

b 2 rows of 6

a 2 rows of 3

c 1 row of 7

REPEATED ADDITION

Repeated addition is adding equal groups or rows together. You can use it to multiply.

Example 1:

4 groups of 5 = 20

5 + 5 + 5 + 5 = 20

4 × 5 = 20

Example 2:

__ rows of __ = __

__ + __ + __ = __

__ × __ = __

How many rows?
How many in each row?

Your turn

Complete:

<u>3</u> rows of <u>3</u> = <u>9</u>

<u>3</u> + <u>3</u> + <u>3</u> = <u>9</u>

<u>3</u> × <u>3</u> = <u>9</u>

b

__ groups of __ = __

__ + __ = __

__ × __ = __

a

__ groups of __ = __

__ + __ = __

__ × __ = __

c

__ rows of __ = __

__ + __ + __ + __ = __

__ × __ = __

1 Draw:

● 2 rows of 3

b 3 groups of 1

a 2 rows of 6

c 5 groups of 4

2 Complete:

2 groups of 4 = _8_

_4_ + _4_ = _8_

_2_ × _4_ = _8_

a

3 groups of 5 = ___

__ + __ + __ = ___

__ × __ = ___

b

5 groups of 2 = ___

__ + __ + __ + __ + __ = ___

__ × __ = ___

c

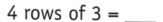

4 rows of 3 = ___

__ + __ + __ + __ = ___

__ × __ = ___

d

5 rows of 1 = __

__ + __ + __ + __ + __ = __

__ × __ = __

e

2 groups of 10 = ___

___ + ___ = ___

__ × ___ = ___

COMMUTATIVE PROPERTY

 Did you know that

$4 \times 2 = 8$ is the same as $2 \times 4 = 8$?

SCAN to watch video

The Commutative Property of multiplication means that you can change the order of the numbers being multiplied and still get the same answer.

This makes it easier to learn your times tables because once you know $2 \times 4 = 8$, you then know $4 \times 2 = 8$.

Example 1:

$2 \times 3 = 3 \times 2$

Both equal 6.

Change the order and you get the same answer.

Example 2:

__ × __ = __ × __

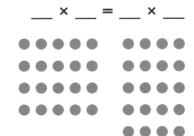

Both equal ___.

Your turn

Complete.

● Show that $3 \times 5 = 5 \times 3$.

Both equal _15_.

a Show that $2 \times 6 = 6 \times 2$.

Both equal ___.

PRACTICE

 1 Complete the following problems.

● 3 × 2 = 2 × 3

b 3 × 6 = 6 × 3

Both equal __6__

Both equal ____

a 2 × 5 = 5 × 2

c 5 × 6 = 6 × 5

Both equal ____

Both equal ____

 2 Match the multiplication problems that show the Commutative Property.

● 1 × 5   6 × 2

a 2 × 6   7 × 2

b 4 × 3   1 × 6

c 5 × 2   3 × 10

d 10 × 3   2 × 5

e 5 × 7   5 × 1

f 6 × 1   3 × 4

g 2 × 7   7 × 5

THE INVERSE OPERATIONS OF MULTIPLICATION AND DIVISION

We know that multiplication is the opposite of division. Another way of saying this is to say multiplication is the inverse operation of division.

So the **inverse** of × is ÷.

SCAN to watch video

Example 1:

Words		Number sentence
3 rows of 4 equals 12	→	3 × 4 = 12
4 groups of 3 equals 12	→	4 × 3 = 12
12 shared into 3 rows equals 4	→	12 ÷ 3 = 4
12 shared into 4 groups equals 3	→	12 ÷ 4 = 3

Example 2:

Words		Number sentence
2 rows of 7 equals 14	→	__ × __ = ___
__ groups of __ equals ___	→	7 × 2 = 14
14 shared into 2 rows equals 7	→	___ ÷ __ = __
___ shared into __ groups equals __	→	14 ÷ 7 = 2

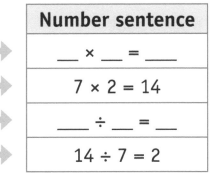

Your turn

Fill in the missing numbers.

Words		Number sentence
3 rows of 2 equals 6	→	3 × ___ = 6
2 groups of __ equals 6	→	2 × ___ = 6
6 shared into 2 rows equals __	→	6 ÷ ___ = 3
__ shared into 3 groups equals 2	→	___ ÷ ___ = 2

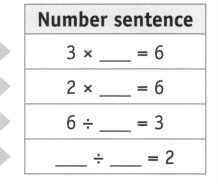

SELF CHECK Mark how you feel

Got it!	Need help...	I don't get it
☐	☐	☐

Check your answers
How many did you get correct?

 1 Complete the following table.

Words		Number sentence
a 5 rows of 3 equals 15	→	
b 3 groups of 5 equals 15	→	
c 15 shared into 3 rows equals 5	→	
d 15 shared into 5 groups equals 3	→	

2 Complete the inverse operations.

● 3 × 4 = 12 → _12_ ÷ _4_ = _3_

a 6 × 3 = 18 → ___ ÷ ___ = ___

b 20 ÷ 2 = 10 → ___ × ___ = ___

c 2 × 9 = 18 → ___ ÷ ___ = ___

d 24 ÷ 2 = 12 → ___ × ___ = ___

e 12 ÷ 1 = 12 → ___ × ___ = ___

f 3 × 7 = 21 → ___ ÷ ___ = ___

g 5 × 7 = 35 → ___ ÷ ___ = ___

 3 Match the inverse operations.

● 3 × 10 = 30   15 ÷ 3 = 5

a 5 × 3 = 15   36 ÷ 12 = 3

b 3 × 8 = 24   20 ÷ 4 = 5

c 5 × 4 = 20   30 ÷ 10 = 3

d 2 × 11 = 22   24 ÷ 8 = 3

e 3 × 12 = 36   22 ÷ 11 = 2

MULTIPLICATION REVIEW

1 How many are in each row?

a ___ in each row

b ___ in each row

c ___ in each row

2 How many are in each group?

a ___ in each group

b ___ in each group

c ___ in each group

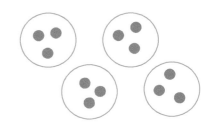

3 Draw the groups, and complete the repeated addition and multiplication.

a 4 groups of 3

b 3 groups of 5

___ + ___ + ___ + ___ = ___

___ + ___ + ___ = ___

___ × ___ = ___

___ × ___ = ___

4 Complete the equations to show the Commutative Property of multiplication.

a 2 × 4 = ___ × ___

e 10 × 2 = ___ × ___

i 1 × 8 = _____

b 3 × 7 = ___ × ___

f 5 × 6 = ___ × ___

j 2 × 7 = _____

c 5 × 8 = ___ × ___

g 1 × 7 = _____

k 8 × 3 = _____

d 3 × 10 = ___ × ___

h 2 × 9 = _____

l 4 × 9 = _____

5 Complete the tables so that the words match each number sentence.

a

Words	Number sentence
___ rows of ___ equals ___	4 × 5 = 20
___ groups of ___ equals ___	5 × 4 = 20
___ shared into ___ rows equals ___	20 ÷
___ shared into ___ groups equals ___	20 ÷

b

Words	Number sentence
___ rows of ___ equals ___	3 × 8 = 24
___ groups of ___ equals ___	
___ shared into ___ rows equals ___	
___ shared into ___ groups equals ___	

6 Write the inverse operation of each multiplication problem.

a 3 × 7 = 21

c 5 × 4 = 20

e 12 × 1 = 12

_____

_____

_____

b 2 × 6 = 12

d 6 × 3 = 18

f 7 × 5 = 35

_____

_____

_____

7 Match the inverse operations.

a 4 × 2 = 8   40 ÷ 4 = 10

b 11 × 2 = 22   60 ÷ 5 = 12

c 12 × 5 = 60   22 ÷ 2 = 11

d 10 × 4 = 40   8 ÷ 2 = 4

GROUPS

When objects are shared equally, each share is called a group.

Example 1: Circle fish to make groups of 2.

There are 5 groups of 2 fish.

Example 2: Circle balls to make groups of 4.

There are 3 groups of 4 balls.

Example 3: Circle stars to make groups of 3.

There are __ groups of __ stars.

> Each group has the same number of things.

Your turn

Circle these items to make groups of 3.

   **a**    **b**

  _2_ groups of 3   ___ groups of 3   ___ groups of 3

SELF CHECK   Mark how you feel

Got it!	Need help...	I don't get it
☐	☐	☐

Check your answers
How many did you get correct?

1 Circle to make:

a groups of 2

____ groups of 2   ____ groups of 2   ____ group of 2

b groups of 3

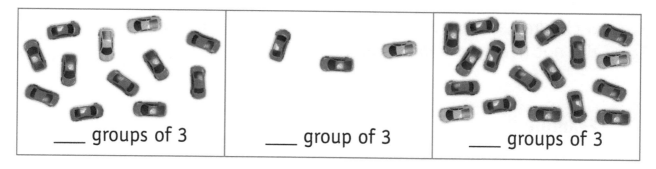

____ groups of 3   ____ group of 3   ____ groups of 3

c groups of 5

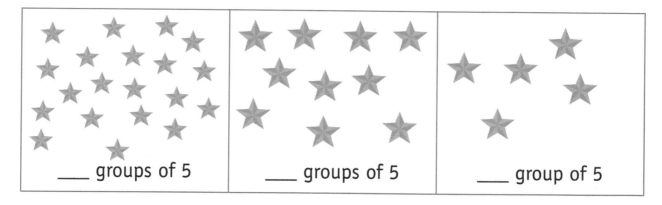

____ groups of 5   ____ groups of 5   ____ group of 5

d groups of 10

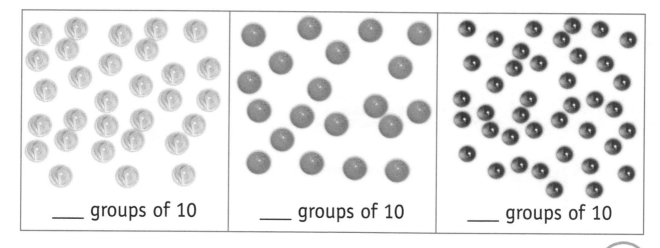

____ groups of 10   ____ groups of 10   ____ groups of 10

DIVISION BY EQUAL SHARES

Equal shares is when an object or a group of objects
is divided equally.

Example 1:

These marbles were not
shared equally among
3 children. Each child
did not get the same number.

Now, the marbles have
been shared equally.
Each child gets 2.

"Sharing equally"
means everyone
gets the same
number.

Example 2:

These ___ cupcakes are shared equally among ___ people.

Each person
gets ___ cupcakes.

Your turn

Draw more items to divide each group into equal shares.

● There are __4__ pencils
in each box.

a There are ___ petals on
each flower.

PRACTICE

1 Draw to make equal shares.

a

b

c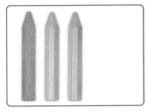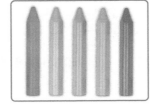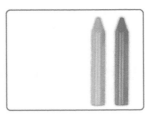

d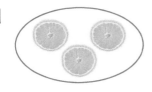

2 Cross out the wrong word.

● ~~equal~~/unequal groups

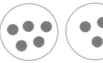

c equal/unequal groups

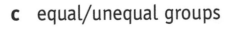

a equal/unequal groups

d equal/unequal groups

b equal/unequal groups

e equal/unequal groups

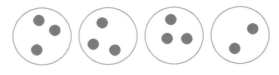

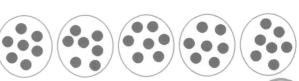

DIVISION BY GROUPING

When you group things equally, you share objects into groups that are the same size.

Example 1:

There are 2 groups and 3 shells in each group.

Example 2:

There are 3 groups and 4 flowers in each group.

> There is the same number of flowers in each group.

Example 3:

There are __ groups and __ beetles in each group.

Your turn

Fill in the missing numbers.

There are _4_ groups and

_3_ candies in each group.

a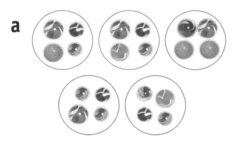

There are ___ groups and

___ marbles in each group.

SELF CHECK Mark how you feel

Got it!	Need help...	I don't get it
☺ ☐	😐 ☐	☹ ☐

Check your answers

How many did you get correct?

PRACTICE

1 Fill in the missing numbers.

There are __2__ groups and

__2__ cupcakes in each group.

b

There are ___ groups and

___ shells in each group.

a

There are ___ groups and

___ strawberries in each group.

c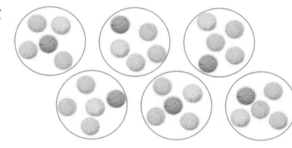

There are ___ groups and

___ balls in each group.

2 Draw groups and items to match the label.

There are 4 groups and 4 triangles in each group.

a _____

There are 5 groups and 3 squares in each group.

b _____

There are 2 groups and 3 circles in each group.

c _____

There are 6 groups and 2 triangles in each group.

DIVISION

SCAN to watch video

Division is the mathematical operation to break up groups or numbers into equal parts. It can be done by sharing or grouping.

In the last chapter, you learned that division is the inverse (or opposite) operation of multiplication.

Example 1: Here are 10 strawberries.

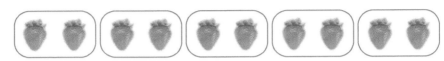

If 5 children get 2 strawberries each, there are 5 groups of 2 strawberries. This can be written as:

This is the number to be shared.

This is the sign used when dividing.

$$10 \div 5 = 2$$

This is how many each group gets.

This is the number of groups.

Example 2: Here are 20 hearts.

If 4 children get __ hearts each, there are __ groups of __ hearts.

This can be written as ___ ÷ ___ = ___.

Make equal groups, and fill in the number sentences.

Your turn

● Here are 16 ■.

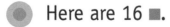

If there are 2 children,

they get _8_ ■ each.

16 ÷ _2_ = 8

a Here are 12 ▲.

If there are 3 children,

they get ___ ▲ each.

12 ÷ ___ = ___

Check your answers
How many did you get correct?

PRACTICE

1 Make equal groups, and fill in the number sentences.

● Put 4 in each group.

There are _4_ groups of 4 hearts.

16 ÷ 4 = _4_

a Put 3 in each group.

There are ___ groups of 3 marbles.

15 ÷ 3 = ___

b Put 5 in each group.

There are ___ groups of 5 stars.

20 ÷ 5 = ___

c Put 2 in each group.

There are ___ groups of 2 balls.

10 ÷ 2 = ___

2 Fill in the missing numbers.

● Make groups of 2.

12 shared with 2 = _6_

12 ÷ 2 = _6_

a Make groups of 5.

25 shared with 5 = ___

25 ÷ 5 = ___

b Make groups of 3.

21 shared with 3 = ___

21 ÷ 3 = ___

c Make groups of 10.

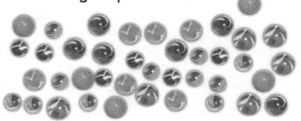

40 shared with 10 = ___

40 ÷ 10 = ___

REMAINDERS

The leftover when a number cannot be divided exactly is called a remainder.

Example 1:

I have 13 jelly beans and share them between 2 people.

1 remainder

$13 \div 2 = 6$ remainder 1

SCAN to watch video

Each person gets 6 jelly beans, and there is 1 remainder (or leftover).

Example 2: I have 14 toy cars and share them among 3 children.

2 remainder

Each child gets __ toy cars, and there are __ remainder.

$14 \div 3 = 4$ remainder 2

Your turn

Solve these division problems.

● Share 10 balls among 3 people.

Each person gets __3__ balls,

and there is __1__ remainder.

$10 \div 3 =$ __3__ remainder __1__

a Share 17 pencils between 2 people.

Each person gets ___ pencils,

and there is ___ remainder.

$17 \div 2 =$ ___ remainder ___

SELF CHECK   Mark how you feel

Got it!	Need help...	I don't get it

Check your answers

How many did you get correct?

1 Solve these division problems.

● I have 16 strawberries, and
I share them among 3 people.

Each person gets _5_ strawberries,

and there is _1_ remainder.

16 ÷ 3 = _5_ remainder _1_

| 1 | remainder

a I have 19 strawberries, and
I share them among 2 people.

Each person gets ___ strawberries,

and there is ___ remainder.

19 ÷ 2 = ___ remainder ___

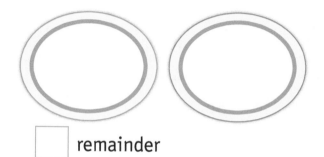

| | remainder

b I have 21 strawberries, and
I share them among 5 people.

Each person gets ___ strawberries,

and there is ___ remainder.

21 ÷ 5 = ___ remainder ___

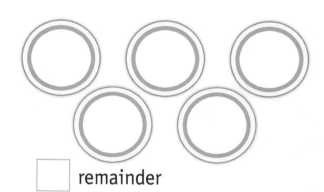

| | remainder

c I have 14 strawberries, and
I share them among 4 people.

Each person gets ___ strawberries,

and there is ___ remainder.

14 ÷ 4 = ___ remainder ___

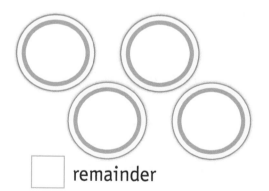

| | remainder

d I have 23 strawberries, and
I share them between 2 people.

Each person gets ___ strawberries,

and there is ___ remainder.

23 ÷ 2 = ___ remainder ___

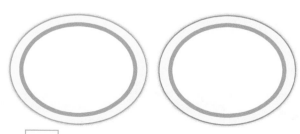

| | remainder

REPEATED SUBTRACTION TO SOLVE DIVISION

Repeated subtraction can be used to solve division problems.

Example 1: 20 ÷ 4 = ___

Start at 20 − 4 = 16
  16 − 4 = 12
  12 − 4 = 8
    8 − 4 = 4   5 times,
    4 − 4 = 0   so the
So, 20 ÷ 4 = 5   answer
                    is 5

Keep repeating until you get to zero.

Example 2: 24 ÷ 3 = ___

Start at 24 − 3 = 21
  ___ − 3 = 18
  ___ − 3 = 15
  ___ − 3 = 12
  ___ − 3 = 9
  ___ − 3 = 6   times,
  ___ − 3 = 3   so the
  ___ − 3 = 0   answer
So, 24 ÷ 3 = ___   is ___

Your turn

Solve using repeated subtraction.

● 12 ÷ 4 = _3_

Start at 12
  12 − 4 = _8_
  _8_ − 4 = _4_   3 times
  _4_ − 4 = _0_

a 15 ÷ 3 = ___

Start at 15
  15 − 3 = ___
  ___ − 3 = ___
  ___ − 3 = ___   ☐ times
  ___ − 3 = ___
  ___ − 3 = ___

PRACTICE

1 Solve using repeated subtraction.

⦿ 24 ÷ 3 = __8__

Start at 24

24 − 3 = 21

21 − 3 = 18

18 − 3 = 15

15 − 3 = 12

12 − 3 = 9

9 − 3 = 6

6 − 3 = 3

3 − 3 = 0

| 8 | times

a 12 ÷ 2 = ___

Start at 12

□ times

b 20 ÷ 5 = ___

Start at 20

□ times

c 30 ÷ 10 = ___

Start at 30

□ times

d 21 ÷ 3 = ___

Start at 21

□ times

e 30 ÷ 5 = ___

Start at 30

□ times

DIVISION REVIEW

 Circle to make groups of 2.

a

b

c

___ groups of ___   ___ groups of ___   ___ groups of ___

 Draw items to make the groups equal.

a

b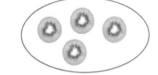

c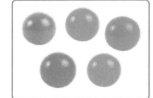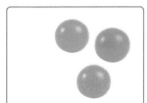

3 **Cross out the wrong word.**

a equal/unequal groups

b equal/unequal groups

c equal/unequal groups

REVIEW

DIVISION

4 Fill in the missing numbers.

a

There are ___ groups and ___ marbles in each group.

b

There are ___ groups and ___ marbles in each group.

c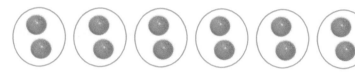

There are ___ groups and ___ marbles in each group.

d

There are ___ groups and ___ marbles in each group.

5 Group the following, then solve the division problems.

a Here are 12 cupcakes.

Show 6 groups of 2.

12 ÷ ___ = ___

b Here are 20 shells.

Show 5 groups of 4.

20 ÷ ___ = ___

c Here are 18 candies.

Show 3 groups of 6.

18 ÷ ___ = ___

d Here are 24 stars.

Show 8 groups of 3.

24 ÷ ___ = ___

© Shell Education

146434—Catch-Up Math

129

REVIEW

6 **Complete.**

a Make groups of 2.

___ shared among ___ = ___

___ ÷ ___ = ___

b Make groups of 3.

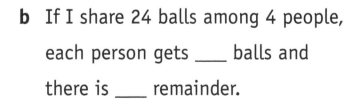

___ shared among ___ = ___

___ ÷ ___ = ___

c Make groups of 5.

___ shared among ___ = ___

___ ÷ ___ = ___

7 **Solve these division problems.**

a If I share 17 balls among 3 people, each person gets ___ balls and there is ___ remainder.

□ remainder

b If I share 24 balls among 4 people, each person gets ___ balls and there is ___ remainder.

□ remainder

8 Solve these division problems using repeated subtraction.

a 24 ÷ 4 = ___

Start at 24

 times

b 12 ÷ 2 = ___

Start at 12

 times

c 15 ÷ 5 = ___

Start at 15

 times

d 35 ÷ 5 = ___

Start at 35

 times

e 40 ÷ 8 = ___

Start at 40

 times

FRACTIONS—HALVES

Numbers that are parts of a whole are called fractions.

When there are only two equal parts, each part is called a half ($\frac{1}{2}$).

Each piece is the same size.

These are NOT two halves.

Example 1: The following circled shapes have been cut into halves.

a

b

c

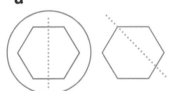
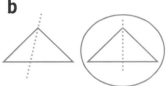
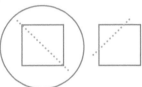

Example 2:

Circle the shape in each pair that has been cut into halves.

a

b

Your turn

Circle the shapes that have been cut into halves.

a   c  e   g

b   d   f 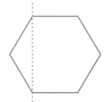 h

PRACTICE

1 Circle the shapes that have been cut into halves.

a  c 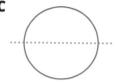 e  g

b  d 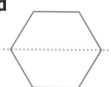 f 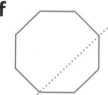 h

2 Draw a line to show how to cut these shapes in half.

a  c 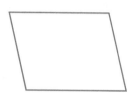 e

b 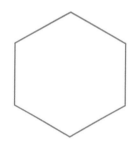 d 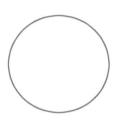 f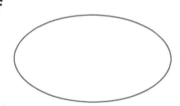

3 Label the shapes that have been cut into halves. Cross out the shapes that are not cut in half.

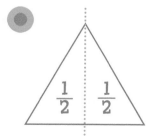 a 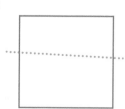 b 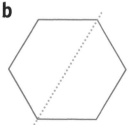 c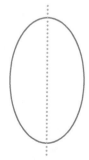

FRACTIONS—QUARTERS AND EIGHTHS

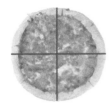 This pizza has been cut into 4 equal parts. Each part is called one-quarter ($\frac{1}{4}$).

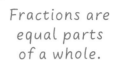 Fractions are equal parts of a whole.

 This pizza has been cut into 8 equal parts. Each part is called one-eighth ($\frac{1}{8}$).

Example 1:
The following shapes have been cut into quarters and eighths.

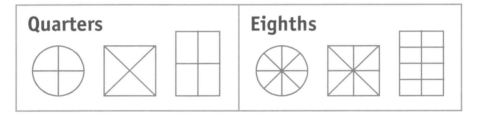

Example 2:
Color one-quarter of this shape.

Example 3:
Color one-eighth of this shape.

Your turn

Circle in blue the shapes that have been cut into quarters.
Circle in red the shapes that have been cut into eighths.

a   c   e   g

b    d   f   h

SELF CHECK Mark how you feel

Got it!	Need help...	I don't get it

Check your answers
How many did you get correct?

PRACTICE

1 Cut these shapes into:

Quarters	Eighths

2 Fill in this table.

	Fraction name	Fraction	Color the fraction
	two-eighths	$\frac{2}{8}$	
a	one-quarter		
b	three-eighths		
c	three-quarters		
d	five-eighths		
e	two-quarters		

3 Divide the shapes into quarters.

a  b 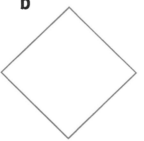 c 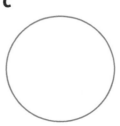 d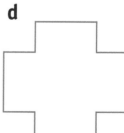

FRACTIONS—THIRDS AND FIFTHS

When a whole is divided into 3 equal parts, each part is called one-third ($\frac{1}{3}$).

When a whole is divided into 5 equal parts, each part is called one-fifth ($\frac{1}{5}$).

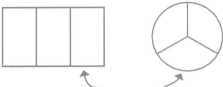

The 3 parts are all the same size.

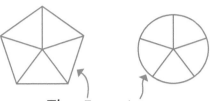

The 5 parts are all the same size.

Example 1:
Color one-third of this shape.

Example 2:
Color one-fifth of this shape.

Example 3:
Color one-third of this shape.

Example 4:
Color one-fifth of this shape.

Remember, each part must be the same size.

Your turn

Circle the shapes in each box that have been cut into thirds and fifths.

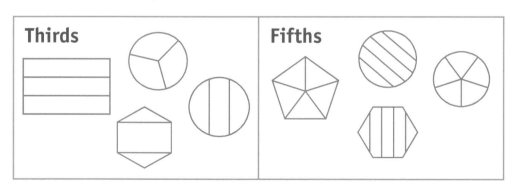

Thirds

Fifths

SELF CHECK Mark how you feel

Got it! ☐   Need help... ☐   I don't get it ☐

Check your answers
How many did you get correct?

PRACTICE

 1 Circle the shapes that have been cut into thirds, and cross out the others.

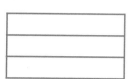 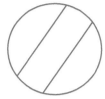

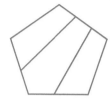  

 2 Color the shapes that have been cut into fifths.

 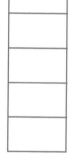 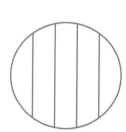

 3 Fill in the table.

	Fraction name	Fraction	Picture
	one-fifth	$\frac{1}{5}$	
a	two-thirds		
b	one-third		
c	four-fifths		

HALF OF A COLLECTION

When a group of things is divided into 2 equal parts, each part is called a half.

Example 1:

I have 8 pencils, and I share them equally with my friend.

My pencils   My friend's pencils

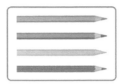 

I group my pencils into 2 equal groups. We each get 4 pencils. Half of 8 = 4.

Each part has the same number of pencils.

Example 2:

I have 10 cupcakes, and I share them equally with my friend.

My cupcakes   My friend's cupcakes

I group the cupcakes into two equal groups.

We each get __ cupcakes. Half of 10 is __.

Your turn

I have 6 balls and share them equally with my friend. How many do we each get?

My balls   My friend's balls

SELF CHECK   Mark how you feel

Got it!   Need help...   I don't get it

Check your answers
How many did you get correct?

PRACTICE

1 Circle half of each group.

a

b

c

2 The following groups have been divided into halves.

 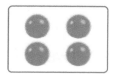

Each box has __4__
of the __8__ balls.

a

Each box has ___
of the ___ balls.

b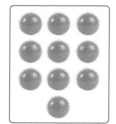

Each box has ___
of the ___ balls.

c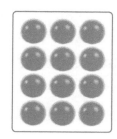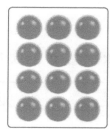

Each box has ___
of the ___ balls.

d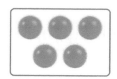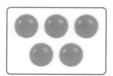

Each box has ___
of the ___ balls.

e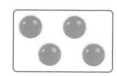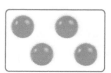

Each box has ___
of the ___ balls.

QUARTERS AND EIGHTHS OF A COLLECTION

When a group of things is divided into 4 equal parts, each part is called one-quarter ($\frac{1}{4}$).

When a group of things is divided into 8 equal parts, each part is called one-eighth ($\frac{1}{8}$).

Example 1: I have 12 pencils and share them between 4 people.

 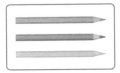 

This is one-quarter of the group.

I group the 12 pencils into 4 equal groups.

Each person gets 3 pencils. $\frac{1}{4}$ of 12 = 3

Example 2: I have 16 balls and share them between 8 friends.

Each person gets 2 balls. $\frac{1}{8}$ of 16 = 2

This is $\frac{1}{8}$ of the collection.

Example 3: If you have 24 apples and share them between 8 people, each person gets ___ apples.

$\frac{1}{8}$ of 24 = ___

Your turn

Fill in the missing numbers.

If you have 8 balls and share them between 4 people, each person gets ___ balls.

$\frac{1}{4}$ of 8 = ___

SELF CHECK Mark how you feel

Got it!	Need help...	I don't get it

Check your answers

How many did you get correct?

1 Share each of the groups into quarters.

a

b

2 Share each of the groups into eighths.

a

b

3 Each group has been divided into quarters or eighths.

  Fill in the missing spaces.

This group has been divided into ____quarters____.

Each box has _4_ of the _16_ marbles. $\frac{1}{4}$ of _16_ = _4_

a

This group has been divided into _____.

Each box has ___ of the ___ marbles. $\frac{1}{8}$ of ___ = ___

b

This group has been divided into _____.

Each box has ___ of the ___ marbles. $\frac{1}{4}$ of ___ = ___

c

This group has been divided into _____.

Each box has ___ of the ___ marbles. $\frac{1}{8}$ of ___ = ___

THIRDS AND FIFTHS OF A COLLECTION

When a group of things is divided into 3 equal parts, each part is called one-third ($\frac{1}{3}$).

When a group of things is divided into 5 equal parts, each part is called one-fifth ($\frac{1}{5}$).

Example 1:
I have 12 candies, and I share them between 3 people.

There are 4 candies in each box. Each share is the same. Each person gets 4 candies.

$\frac{1}{3}$ of 12 = 4

Example 2:
I have 15 strawberries, and I share them between 5 people.

There are 3 strawberries on each plate. Each share is the same. Each person gets 3 strawberries.

$\frac{1}{5}$ of 15 = 3

Example 3: I have 9 buttons, and I share them between 3 people.

$\frac{1}{3}$ of 9 = ___

Your turn

Complete.

a I have 18 strawberries, and I share them between 3 people.

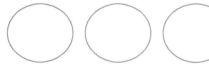

Each person gets ___ strawberries.

$\frac{1}{3}$ of 18 = ___

b I have 25 candies, and I share them between 5 people.

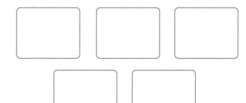

Each person gets ___ candies.

$\frac{1}{5}$ of 25 = ___

SELF CHECK Mark how you feel

Got it!	Need help...	I don't get it
☺ ☐	😐 ☐	😠 ☐

Check your answers
How many did you get correct?

PRACTICE

FRACTIONS

1 Divide each of these groups into thirds.

  $\frac{1}{3}$ of 9 fish = __3__ fish

a  $\frac{1}{3}$ of 6 fish = ___ fish

b $\frac{1}{3}$ of 15 fish = ___ fish

c  $\frac{1}{3}$ of 3 fish = ___ fish

2 Divide each of these groups into fifths.

     $\frac{1}{5}$ of 15 cars = __3__ cars

a  $\frac{1}{5}$ of 10 cars = ___ cars

b $\frac{1}{5}$ of 20 cars = ___ cars

c $\frac{1}{5}$ of 5 cars = ___ cars

3 Each group has been shared into thirds or fifths.
Fill in the missing numbers.

⦿ 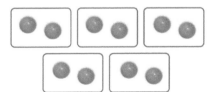   Each box has __3__ of the __9__ marbles.
$\frac{1}{3}$ of __9__ marbles = __3__ marbles

a 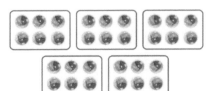   Each box has ___ of the ___ marbles.
$\frac{1}{3}$ of ___ marbles = ___ marbles

b   Each box has ___ of the ___ marbles.
$\frac{1}{5}$ of ___ marbles = ___ marbles

c   Each box has ___ of the ___ marbles.
$\frac{1}{5}$ of ___ marbles = ___ marbles

© Shell Education

146434—Catch-Up Math   **143**

COMPARING FRACTIONS

This is a fraction wall. It makes comparing fractions easy.

1 whole							
$\frac{1}{2}$				$\frac{1}{2}$			
$\frac{1}{4}$		$\frac{1}{4}$		$\frac{1}{4}$		$\frac{1}{4}$	
$\frac{1}{8}$	$\frac{1}{8}$	$\frac{1}{8}$	$\frac{1}{8}$	$\frac{1}{8}$	$\frac{1}{8}$	$\frac{1}{8}$	$\frac{1}{8}$
$\frac{1}{3}$		$\frac{1}{3}$			$\frac{1}{3}$		
$\frac{1}{5}$		$\frac{1}{5}$	$\frac{1}{5}$		$\frac{1}{5}$		$\frac{1}{5}$

SCAN to watch video

The larger the bottom number, the smaller the fraction.

One-third ($\frac{1}{3}$) is larger than one-eighth ($\frac{1}{8}$).

One-fifth ($\frac{1}{5}$) is smaller than one-half ($\frac{1}{2}$).

Example 1: Write a fraction that is smaller than $\frac{1}{4}$. $\boxed{\frac{1}{8}}$

Example 2: Write a fraction that is smaller than $\frac{3}{5}$. $\boxed{\frac{2}{5}}$

Example 3: Write a fraction that is smaller than $\frac{1}{2}$. $\boxed{}$

Example 4: Write a fraction that is smaller than $\frac{3}{8}$. $\boxed{}$

Your turn

Use the fraction wall, and write *True* or *False*.

● $\frac{2}{3}$ is smaller than $\frac{1}{2}$ _____False_____

a $\frac{3}{8}$ is larger than $\frac{1}{2}$ _____

b $\frac{5}{8}$ is smaller than $\frac{3}{5}$ _____

c $\frac{4}{5}$ is larger than $\frac{7}{8}$ _____

PRACTICE

1 Using the fraction wall, place these fractions on the number line.

● $\frac{1}{4}, \frac{3}{8}, \frac{7}{8}, \frac{1}{2}$

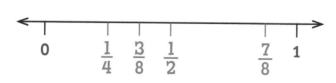

a $\frac{1}{4}, \frac{1}{5}, \frac{1}{8}, \frac{1}{3}$

To help, look on the fraction wall to see how big the fractions are.

b $\frac{3}{4}, \frac{2}{5}, \frac{3}{8}, \frac{2}{3}$

2 Fill in the following using fractions.

● 3 pizza slices out of 8 = $\frac{3}{8}$ eaten and $\frac{5}{8}$ left

a 2 pizza slices out of 8 = $\frac{}{8}$ eaten and $\frac{}{8}$ left

b 7 pizza slices out of 8 = $\frac{}{8}$ eaten and $\frac{}{8}$ left

3 Order these fractions from largest to smallest.

● $\frac{5}{10}, \frac{4}{10}, \frac{2}{10}, \frac{1}{10}, \frac{7}{10}$ $\frac{7}{10}, \frac{5}{10}, \frac{4}{10}, \frac{2}{10}, \frac{1}{10}$

a $\frac{3}{10}, \frac{5}{10}, \frac{6}{10}, \frac{8}{10}, \frac{1}{10}$ _____

b $\frac{34}{100}, \frac{24}{100}, \frac{17}{100}, \frac{5}{100}, \frac{13}{100}$ _____

c $\frac{1}{2}, \frac{1}{3}, \frac{1}{4}, \frac{1}{5}, \frac{1}{8}$ _____

4 Color in the fractions, then order them from smallest (1) to largest (5).

 $\frac{1}{4}$ $\frac{1}{3}$ $\frac{1}{2}$ $\frac{1}{5}$ $\frac{1}{8}$

5 Compare the fractions using < and >.
< means "less than," > means "greater than."

$\frac{1}{3}$ _<_ $\frac{1}{2}$ c $\frac{1}{3}$ ___ $\frac{1}{5}$ f $\frac{3}{4}$ ___ $\frac{7}{8}$

a $\frac{1}{4}$ ___ $\frac{3}{8}$ d $\frac{1}{4}$ ___ $\frac{3}{4}$ g $\frac{1}{2}$ ___ $\frac{1}{3}$

b $\frac{1}{8}$ ___ $\frac{1}{2}$ e $\frac{7}{8}$ ___ $\frac{2}{5}$ h $\frac{5}{8}$ ___ $\frac{1}{2}$

The fraction wall will help you!

6 Circle the fraction of each group of 24 fish.

a

b

c

$\frac{1}{4}$ of 24 fish

= ___ fish

$\frac{1}{3}$ of 24 fish

= ___ fish

$\frac{1}{2}$ of 24 fish

= ___ fish

d ___ is the biggest fraction of fish.

e ___ is the smallest fraction of fish.

7 Circle the largest fraction in each group.

⬤ $\frac{1}{4}$, $\frac{1}{8}$, $\boxed{\frac{3}{4}}$ c $\frac{4}{5}$, $\frac{2}{10}$, $\frac{9}{10}$ f $\frac{1}{4}$, $\frac{2}{3}$, $\frac{6}{10}$

a $\frac{1}{2}$, $\frac{1}{3}$, $\frac{2}{5}$ d $\frac{1}{4}$, $\frac{1}{3}$, $\frac{9}{10}$ g $\frac{3}{4}$, $\frac{2}{5}$, $\frac{3}{8}$

b $\frac{3}{5}$, $\frac{7}{8}$, $\frac{3}{4}$ e $\frac{3}{10}$, $\frac{4}{5}$, $\frac{6}{8}$ h $\frac{3}{5}$, $\frac{7}{8}$, $\frac{2}{3}$

8 Cross out the smallest fraction in each group.

⬤ $\frac{1}{2}$, $\frac{3}{8}$, $\frac{2}{4}$ c $\frac{3}{10}$, $\frac{2}{5}$, $\frac{7}{8}$ f $\frac{5}{8}$, $\frac{1}{2}$, $\frac{2}{5}$

a $\frac{2}{5}$, $\frac{3}{4}$, $\frac{3}{8}$ d $\frac{5}{10}$, $\frac{3}{4}$, $\frac{2}{5}$ g $\frac{4}{5}$, $\frac{2}{4}$, $\frac{6}{8}$

b $\frac{1}{3}$, $\frac{3}{5}$, $\frac{3}{8}$ e $\frac{2}{3}$, $\frac{3}{8}$, $\frac{3}{4}$ h $\frac{7}{8}$, $\frac{2}{3}$, $\frac{3}{8}$

FRACTIONS REVIEW

1 Circle the shapes with halves red, quarters blue, eighths green, thirds yellow, and fifths orange.

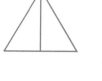
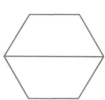

2 Color in the fractions.

a	b	c	d	e
$\frac{2}{3}$	$\frac{3}{5}$	$\frac{3}{4}$	$\frac{1}{2}$	$\frac{7}{8}$

3 Match the labels to the correct fraction and picture.

a two-fifths $\qquad$ $\frac{2}{5}$

b five-eighths $\qquad$ $\frac{1}{4}$

c one-third $\qquad$ $\frac{5}{8}$

d one-quarter $\qquad$ $\frac{1}{3}$

REVIEW

4 Circle one-half of each group, and fill in the missing numbers.

a

$\frac{1}{2}$ of ____ = ____

b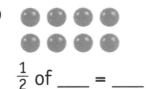

$\frac{1}{2}$ of ____ = ____

c

$\frac{1}{2}$ of ____ = ____

d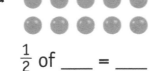

$\frac{1}{2}$ of ____ = ____

e

$\frac{1}{2}$ of ____ = ____

f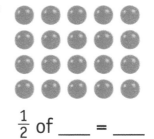

$\frac{1}{2}$ of ____ = ____

5 Divide each of these groups in half.

a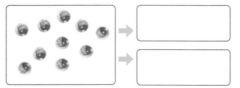

Each box has ____

of the ____ marbles.

b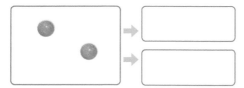

Each box has ____

of the ____ marbles.

c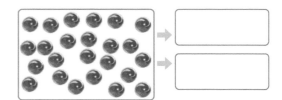

Each box has ____

of the ____ marbles.

d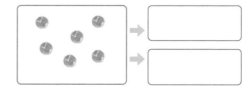

Each box has ____

of the ____ marbles.

6 Circle one-quarter of each group, and fill in the missing numbers.

a

$\frac{1}{4}$ of ____ = ____

b

$\frac{1}{4}$ of ____ = ____

c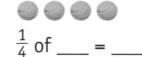

$\frac{1}{4}$ of ____ = ____

d

$\frac{1}{4}$ of ____ = ____

7 Divide each of these groups into quarters.

a
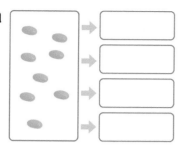

Each bag has ___ jelly beans.

b
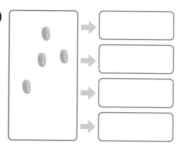

Each bag has ___ jelly beans.

c
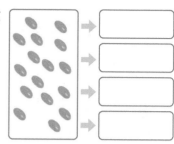

Each bag has ___ jelly beans.

8 Which groups have been shared into eighths? Draw an *X* on them.

a

d

b

e

c

9 Share these marbles into thirds.

$\frac{1}{3}$ of ___ marbles = ___ marbles

10 Share these marbles into fifths.

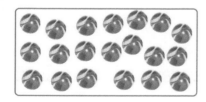

$\frac{1}{5}$ of ___ marbles = ___ marbles

11 Write these numbers from smallest to largest.

a $\frac{3}{4}$, $\frac{7}{8}$, 1 whole, $\frac{2}{5}$ _____

b $\frac{2}{3}$, $\frac{4}{5}$, $\frac{6}{8}$, $\frac{3}{8}$ _____

12 Write these fractions on the number line.

a $\frac{1}{8}, \frac{1}{4}, \frac{2}{3}, \frac{7}{8}$

0   1

b $\frac{2}{5}, \frac{1}{4}, \frac{3}{4}, \frac{1}{2}$

0   1

c $\frac{3}{3}, \frac{3}{5}, \frac{1}{8}, \frac{1}{4}$

0   1

d $\frac{1}{3}, \frac{1}{2}, \frac{3}{4}, \frac{7}{8}$

0   1

13 Use > (greater than) or < (less than) to compare the fractions.

a $\frac{2}{4}$ ___ $\frac{3}{8}$ d $\frac{1}{2}$ ___ $\frac{2}{3}$ g $\frac{1}{5}$ ___ $\frac{1}{4}$

b $\frac{2}{8}$ ___ $\frac{1}{2}$ e $\frac{6}{8}$ ___ $\frac{1}{2}$ h $\frac{1}{3}$ ___ $\frac{1}{2}$

c $\frac{3}{5}$ ___ $\frac{7}{8}$ f $\frac{4}{5}$ ___ $\frac{1}{4}$ i $\frac{7}{8}$ ___ $\frac{3}{4}$

14 Here are 12 fish.

$\frac{1}{4}$ of 12 fish = ___ fish

$\frac{1}{3}$ of 12 fish = ___ fish

$\frac{1}{2}$ of 12 fish = ___ fish

15 Circle the largest fraction in each group, and cross out the smallest fraction.

a $\frac{1}{3}, \frac{3}{5}, \frac{4}{8}$ d $\frac{4}{5}, \frac{1}{2}, \frac{7}{8}$ g $\frac{2}{3}, \frac{3}{4}, \frac{7}{8}$

b $\frac{1}{2}, \frac{3}{4}, \frac{2}{5}$ e $\frac{1}{5}, \frac{5}{8}, \frac{3}{4}$ h $\frac{1}{4}, \frac{1}{2}$, 1 whole

c $\frac{2}{3}, \frac{1}{4}, \frac{3}{5}$ f $\frac{3}{5}, \frac{7}{8}, \frac{3}{4}$

DATA AND TABLES

Data is information. A table is often used to display data.

Example 1:

The following table shows the data collected in answer to the question:
What are the favorite colors of the students in Room 3?

Room 3's Favorite Colors ← This is the information being collected.

Color	Tally	Total
Red	||||	4
Pink	‖‖‖	5
Blue	‖‖‖ ‖‖‖ |	11
Black	‖‖‖	5
		25

← After we count the tallies, we write in the total.

↑ These are called tally marks.

From this table, we can get lots of information.

• Twenty-five students were surveyed
  (asked what their favorite colors were).

• The most popular color was blue.

• The least popular color was red.

• Both pink and black were equally popular.

How many students said their favorite color was

a red? _4_   **c** blue? _11_

b pink? _5_   **d** black? _5_

We count the tallies or look at the total in the table.

Example 2: Count the tally marks, and record the totals.

Birds Seen by Ben on Saturday

Bird	Tally	Total
Blue Jay	̶H̶H̶ I	
Crow	̶H̶H̶ ̶H̶H̶ I	
Cardinal	̶H̶H̶ I	
Dove	̶H̶H̶	
Sparrow	̶H̶H̶ ̶H̶H̶	
Seagull	̶H̶H̶ ̶H̶H̶ IIII	

Your turn

Look at the data in this table.

Favorite Foods

Food	Tally	Total
Pizza	̶H̶H̶ I	6
Tacos	̶H̶H̶ III	8
Pasta	̶H̶H̶ I	6
Fish and chips	II	2
		22

Complete the sentences based on the data in the table.

a The most popular food was _____.

b The least popular food was _____.

c Both _____ and _____ were equally popular.

d There were _____ people surveyed.

SELF CHECK   Mark how you feel

Got it! ☐   Need help... ☐   I don't get it ☐

Check your answers
How many did you get correct?

© Shell Education

1 Fill in the missing information in the tables.

a   Room 4's Favorite Sports

Sport	Tally	Total
Soccer	~~||||~~ ||	
Football	~~||||~~ |||	
Tennis		5
Basketball		3
		23

b   Room 4's Favorite Ice Cream

Ice Cream	Tally	Total
Chocolate		8
Vanilla		10
Strawberry			
Caramel	||||	
Mint	||	
		25

c   Room 4's Favorite Fruits

Fruit	Tally	Total
Apple	|||	
Mango		14
Banana	~~||||~~ |||	
Watermelon		6
Grapes	||	

Adon asked a group of people what their favorite days of the week were, and the results are shown in the table.

Favorite Days of the Week

Day	Tally	Total
Monday		0
Tuesday	||	2
Wednesday	||||	4
Thursday	||||	4
Friday	⊬⊬ ||	7
Saturday	⊬⊬ ||||	9
Sunday	⊬⊬ ⊬⊬ ||	12
		38

Complete the following using the data in the table.

a The most popular day of the week was _____.

b The least popular day of the week was _____.

c The days which were equally popular were _____ and _____.

d The difference between the number of people who chose Sunday and those who chose Tuesday is _____.

e The difference between the number of people who chose Saturday and those who chose Thursday is _____.

f How many people chose Monday? _____

g How many people chose Friday? _____

PICTURE GRAPHS

A picture graph uses pictures to represent data.
A key is used to explain what the pictures mean.

Example:

Room 4 Birthdays

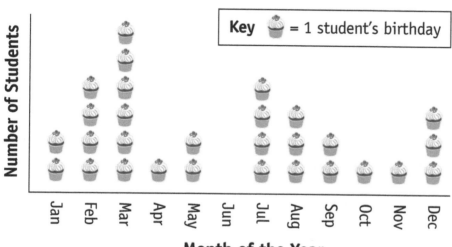

Key = 1 student's birthday

Number of Students

Jan Feb Mar Apr May Jun Jul Aug Sep Oct Nov Dec

Month of the Year

The key tells us 🧁 = 1 student's birthday.

We can see the month with the most birthdays is March.
It has 6 cupcakes, which means 6 students in Room 4
have their birthdays in March.

No students have birthdays in June.

Answer these questions.

a How many students have their birthdays in January? _____

b Which three months have exactly one student's birthday?

_____

c Write the months that have the same number of birthdays.

• January and _____

• February and _____

• December and _____

1 The following picture graph shows the types of vehicles that passed Busy Street Public School.

Types of Vehicles That Passed Busy Street Public School

Motorcycle	⊕
Car	⊕ ⊕ ⊕ ⊕ ⊕ ⊕ ⊕
Truck	⊕ ⊕ ⊕
Bus	⊕ ⊕ ⊕ ⊕

Key
⊕ = 1 type of vehicle

Answer these questions.

a How many cars passed? _____

b How many buses passed? _____

c How many more cars passed than motorcycles? _____

d _____ went past the most often.

e _____ went past the least often.

2 Use the information in the table to complete the picture graph.

Room 5's Favorite Ways to Travel

Vehicles	Total
Car	6
Bus	2
Train	8
Bike	5
Walk	6
	27

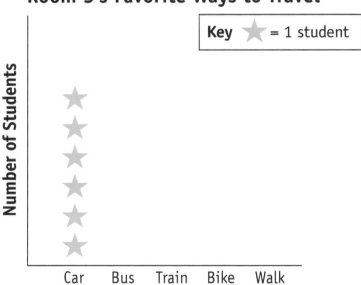

Room 5's Favorite Ways to Travel

Key ★ = 1 student

SELF CHECK   Mark how you feel

Got it!   Need help...   I don't get it

Check your answers
How many did you get correct?

156   146434—Catch-Up Math   © Shell Education

PRACTICE

1 Lucas recorded all the activities he did in May on the calendar.

MAY

Sunday	Monday	Tuesday	Wednesday	Thursday	Friday	Saturday
	1 Swim X	2 Band X	3 Art	4 Soccer	5	6 Soccer
7 Surfing	8 Swim	9 Band	10 Art	11 Soccer	12 Drama	13 Soccer
14	15 Swim	16 Band	17 Art	18 Soccer	19 Drama	20 Soccer
21 Surfing	22 Swim	23 Band	24 Art	25 Soccer	26 Drama	27 Soccer
28	29 Swim	30 Band	31 Art			

Record this data using tallies in the table.
Put an X on each activity, then record it in the table.
The first two have been done for you.

Lucas's Activities in May

Activity	Tally	Total
Surfing		
Swim	/	
Band	/	
Art		
Soccer		
Drama		

2 Color one ☐ for every activity Lucas does.

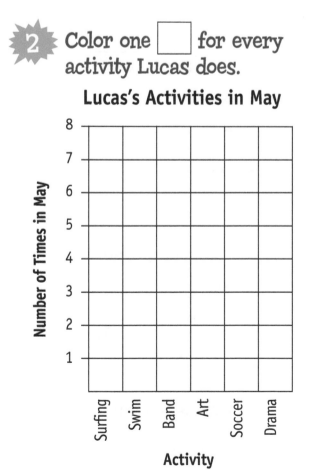

Lucas's Activities in May

3 Answer these questions using the data in the graph.

a What activity did Lucas do most often? _____

b What activity did Lucas do least often? _____

c How many more days did Lucas go to soccer than to art? _____

d How many days did Lucas attend band? _____

 4 The children in Room 12 made a graph of the pets they own.
The girls' pets are shown in red, and the boys' pets are shown in blue.

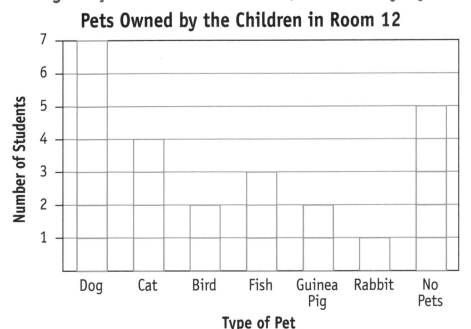

Answer these questions using the data in the graph.

a How many boys have pet cats? ____

b How many girls have pet dogs? ____

c How many students have pet fish? ____

d What is the most popular pet? _____

e How many students have no pet? ____

f How many boys are in the class? ____

g How many students are in the class? ____

h What is the difference between the number of
students who have dogs and those who have fish? _____

5 This picture graph shows how many books each student read in Semester 1.

How Many Books Students Read in Semester 1

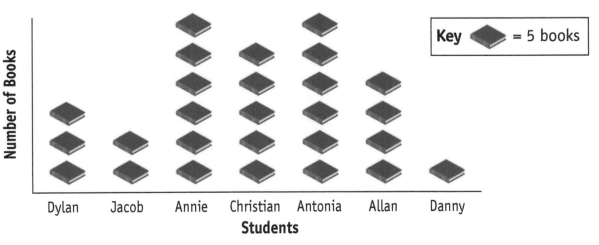

Key ◆ = 5 books

Look at the graph, and complete the table.

Number of Books Read in Semester 1

Name	Tally	Total
Dylan		
Jacob		
Annie		
Christian		
Antonia		
Allan		
Danny		

Answer these questions using the data in the table.

a How many books did Allan read? _____

b Who read the smallest number of books? _____

c How many books did Dylan and Jacob read altogether? _____

d Which two students read the same number of books?

_____ and _____

6 Tim rolled a number cube, and he graphed his results in this picture graph.

Rolls

Tally Tim's results in this table.

Rolls

Number	Tally	Total
⚀		
⚁		
⚂		
⚃		
⚄		
⚅		

Answer these questions using the data in the table.

a What number did Tim roll most often? ____

b What number did Tim roll least often? ____

c How many times was rolled? ____

d How many more times was ⚀ rolled than ⚅? ____

e How many times did Tim roll the number cube? ____

7 Room 15 surveyed the colors of the cars that passed their school. They tallied their results.

Cars That Passed Our School

Color	Tally	Total
Red	|||	3
Black	ﬞﬞ﷼ﬞ﷼	11
Silver	﷼﷼ ||||	9
White	﷼﷼ |||	8
Blue			1
		32

a Draw and color one block for every two cars that passed.

Cars That Passed Our School

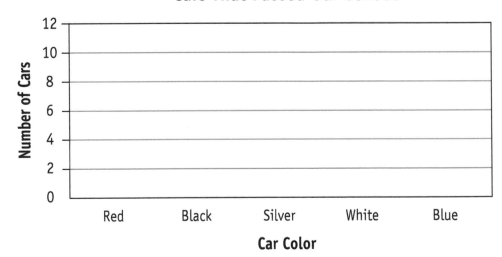

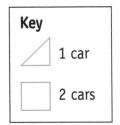

Key

◸ 1 car

▢ 2 cars

b Write three things you learned from this survey.

- _____

_____

- _____

_____

- _____

_____

BAR GRAPHS

A bar graph is a graph that shows the data in columns that can be vertical or horizontal.

Example 1: This is a vertical bar graph.

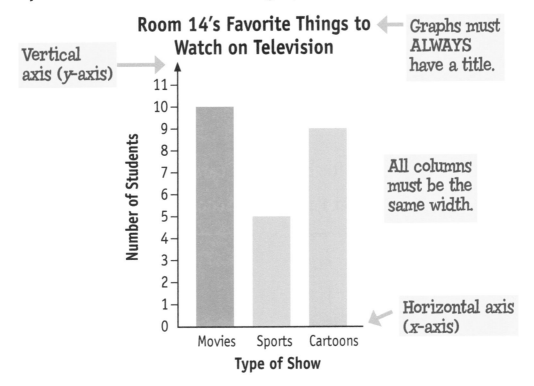

Vertical axis (y-axis)

Graphs must ALWAYS have a title.

All columns must be the same width.

Horizontal axis (x-axis)

Example 2: Complete this horizontal bar graph to show the same data as in Example 1.

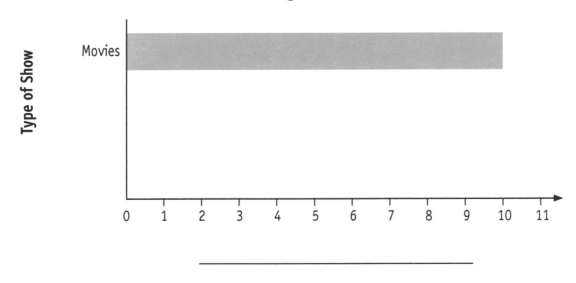

Room 14's Favorite Things to Watch on Television

Look at the bar graph, and answer the questions.

How Students in Room 20 Travel to School

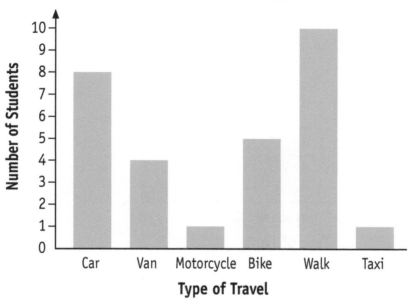

a What is the most common way students in Room 20 travel to school?

_____

b Which type of travel do 8 students use?

_____

c How many students travel to school by taxi? _____

d How many students ride their bikes to school? _____

e Which two methods do the same number of students use?

_____ and _____

f How many more students walk than ride bikes? _____

g How many students are included in the data? _____

Check your answers
How many did you get correct?

PRACTICE

1

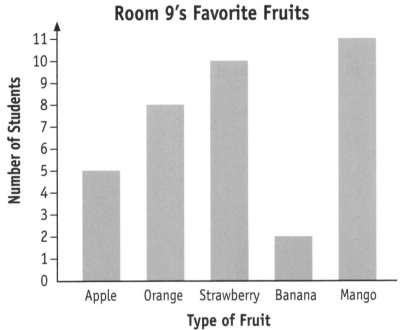

Room 9's Favorite Fruits

Use the bar graph to answer these questions.

a What fruit was the least popular? _____

b How many students in Room 9 chose strawberry? ____

c The most popular fruit was _____.

d What was the difference between the most popular and the least popular fruit? ____

e What was the difference between apples and oranges? ____

2 Use the information from the bar graph to fill in the table.

Room 9's Favorite Fruits

Type of Fruit	Tally	Total
Apple	⊪⊩	5

3 Now, create a horizontal bar graph of Room 9's favorite fruits. Be sure to label your graph and the axes.

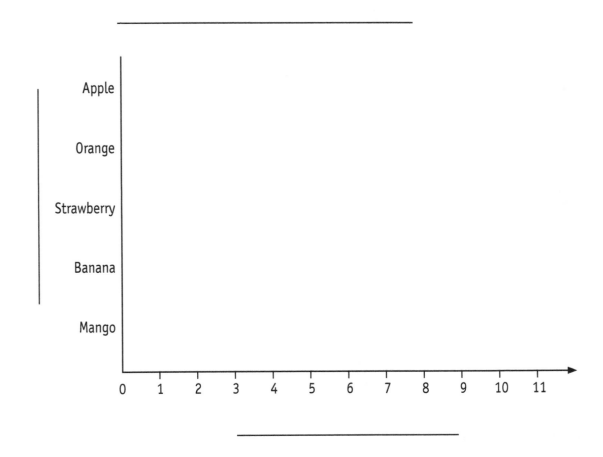

4 Write three questions you could ask a friend using the information in the graph above.

- _____

  _____

- _____

  _____

- _____

  _____

5 The graph shows how many boys and girls in Maytown liked different types of movies.

Types of Movies Liked by Children in Maytown

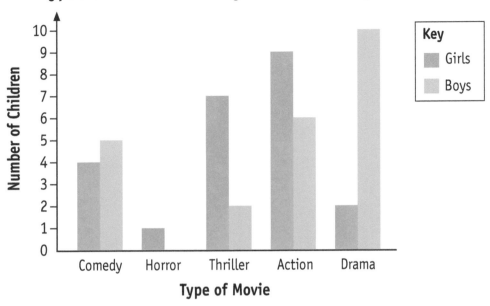

Answer these questions using the data in the graph.

a The most popular movies for girls were _____.

b The least popular movies for boys were _____.

c _____ for girls and _____ for boys were equally liked.

d Girls liked comedy movies more/less than boys.

e Boys liked thriller movies more/less than girls.

f The difference between the number of boys and girls who liked drama movies is _____.

DATA REVIEW

1 Fill in the missing information from this table, then answer the questions.

Room 12's Favorite Colors

Color	Tally	Total
Black	||	
Red		5
Orange		3
Blue		10

a How many students chose black as their favorite color? _____

b What's the favorite color of the greatest number of students in Room 12?

   _____

c What was the least popular color in Room 12? _____

d What is the difference between the number of students who chose red and and those who chose blue? _____

2 This table shows the favorite fruits of the students in Room 15. Write the total of each type of fruit.

Room 15's Favorite Fruits

Type of Fruit	Tally	Total
Banana	||	
Mango	~~||||~~	
Cherries	~~||||~~ ~~||||~~	
Watermelon	~~||||~~ ~~||||~~ ||	
		29

REVIEW

3 Construct a picture graph showing all the information from the table in question 2.

Title: _____

Key △ = 1 piece of fruit

4 Tony made this table from data he collected.

Favorite Cars

Car type	Tally	Total
Nassin	ꟷꟷꟷ	5
Mani	ꟷꟷꟷ ꟷꟷꟷ	8
Tayata	ꟷꟷꟷ	3
Fard	ꟷꟷ	2
Nitsubyshi	ꟷ	1
WV	ꟷꟷꟷꟷ	4

Construct the following graphs using Tony's table.

Vertical bar graph

_____

Horizontal bar graph

_____

INFORMAL UNITS

You can measure and compare lengths using small, equal units that are exactly the same length.

bricks   paper clips   shoes

Examples: Complete the measurements.

a

The pencil is a bit longer than _6_ bricks.

b

The spoon is as long as __ paper clips.

c

This table is a bit shorter than __ shoes.

 Your turn

> Measure exactly from one end, with no gaps and no overlaps.

Complete.

● The finger is _2_ bricks long.

a The paintbrush is __ bricks long.

b The fork is __ bricks long.

c The crayon is shorter / longer than the paintbrush.

d The finger is the shortest / longest.

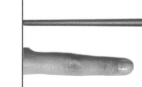

PRACTICE

1 Write the length in paper clips for each arrow.

= __6__ paper clips

= ____ paper clips

= ____ paper clips

= ____ paper clips

2 Write *shorter* or *longer* to complete the sentences.

The red arrow is ___longer___ than the orange arrow.

a The orange arrow is _____ than the red arrow.

b The blue arrow is _____ than the orange arrow.

c The green arrow is _____ than the blue arrow.

3 Use the lines to complete the following.

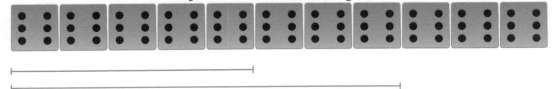

The ___green___ line is the longest.

a The _____ line is the shortest.

b The blue line is ___ number cubes long.

c The orange line is ___ number cubes long.

d The _____ line is 11 number cubes long.

e The difference in length between the
longest line and the shortest line is ___ number cubes.

4 Number the boxes from 1 for the shortest pencil to 3 for the longest pencil.

[ ]

[1]

[ ]

5 Circle the correct measurements.

● The green pencil is 3 bricks / (4 bricks) long.

a The yellow pencil is 3 bricks / 5 bricks long.

b The orange pencil is 4 bricks / 5 bricks long.

c The difference in length between the green pencil and the orange pencil is 1 brick / 2 bricks.

d The difference in length between the yellow pencil and the orange pencil is 3 bricks / 2 bricks.

6 Complete the following.

● The color of the shortest pencil is __yellow__.

a The color of the longest pencil is _____.

b The green pencil is longer than the _____ pencil.

c If I had a red pencil that was shorter than the yellow pencil, how many bricks long could it be? _____

d If I had a black pencil that was 6 bricks long, would it be shorter or longer than the orange pencil? _____

e If I had a pink pencil that was 4 bricks long, would it be shorter or longer than the yellow pencil? _____

METERS AND FEET

A meter is 100 centimeters. We write the symbol for meter as m. A foot is 12 inches. We write the symbol for feet as ft.

We use meters and feet to measure big things.

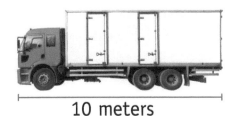

10 meters

4 meters

16 feet

45 feet

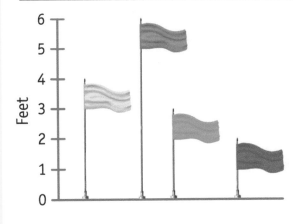

The yellow flag is 4 feet (4 ft.) tall.
The red flag is 6 feet (6 ft.) tall.
The green flag is 3 feet (3 ft.) tall.
The purple flag is 2 feet (2 ft.) tall.

50 centimeters is half a meter.

Look at these things that have been measured.

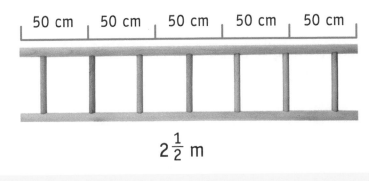

50 cm 50 cm 50 cm 50 cm 50 cm

$2\frac{1}{2}$ m

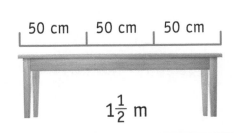

50 cm 50 cm 50 cm

$1\frac{1}{2}$ m

Examples: Use blue to color the items best measured in feet.

a ▩ truck   e ☐ hand   i ☐ book

b ☐ laptop   f ☐ bus   j ☐ bicycle

c ☐ calculator   g ☐ car   k ☐ pencil case

d ☐ horse   h ☐ cup   l ☐ finger

Your turn

Use the doors to answer the following questions.

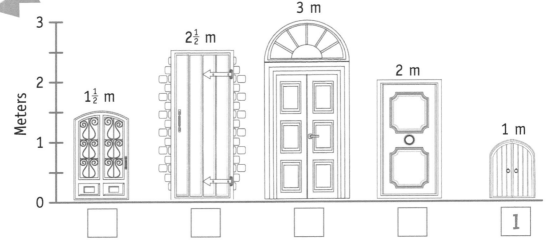

a Number the doors from shortest (1) to tallest (5).

b Color the tallest door green and the shortest door red.

c Use blue to color the door that is $2\frac{1}{2}$ m high.

d Use yellow to color the door that is 2 m high.

e Use orange to color the door that is $1\frac{1}{2}$ m high.

f What is the difference in height between the tallest door and the shortest door? _____

PRACTICE

1 Use the scale at the left to find the heights of the buildings in Toyhouse Town. Label each building with the height in feet.

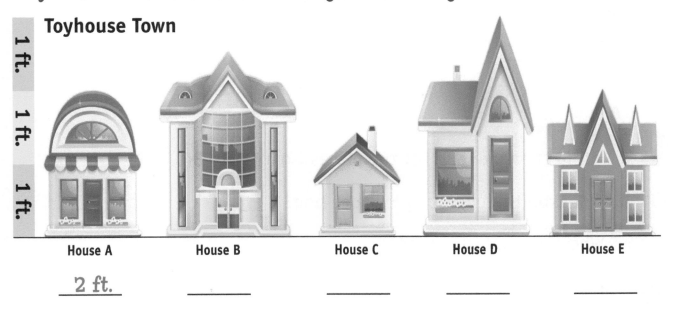

Toyhouse Town

1 ft. 1 ft. 1 ft. 1 ft.

House A   House B   House C   House D   House E

__2 ft.__   _____   _____   _____   _____

2 Use Toyhouse Town to answer the following questions.

⦿ The tallest house is House <u>D</u>.

a The shortest house is House __.

b House E is ____ feet high.

c House B is ____ feet high.

d House C is ____ feet high.

e The difference in height between House D and House A is ___ ft.

f House A and House ___ are the same height.

In a high jump competition, the following measurements were taken.

Name	Measurement (m)	Measurement (cm)	Place
Ally	$1\frac{1}{2}$ m	150 cm	
Hazel	1 m		
Amber	2 m		1st

a Fill in the table and list the places from 1st to 3rd.

b Who won the high jump competition? _____

c Who came in last place? _____

 List things that match each description.

Things less than 1 ft.	Things about 1 ft.	Things more than 1 ft.

5 List things that match each description.

Things less than 1 m	Things about 1 m	Things more than 1 m

CENTIMETERS AND INCHES

A centimeter is smaller than a meter. We use cm to write centimeters. An inch is smaller than a foot. We can use in. to write inches.

This ruler shows inches and centimeters.

SCAN to watch video

Examples: Measure these objects.

a   <u>3</u> in.

b   ___ in.

c   ___ cm

d   ___ in.

e   ___ cm

Your turn

Use the ruler and objects above to answer the questions.

Which object is longest? <u>paintbrush</u>

a   Number the objects to order them from shortest (1) to longest (5).

☐ crayon   ☐ paintbrush   ☐ pencil   ☐ eraser   ☐ highlighter

b   How much longer is the paintbrush than the eraser? _____

c   How much shorter is the highlighter than the pencil? _____

d   Is the highlighter longer or shorter than the crayon? _____

SELF CHECK   Mark how you feel

Got it! ☐   Need help... ☐   I don't get it ☐

Check your answers
How many did you get correct? ☐

PRACTICE

1 Measure the objects in centimeters.

a _____   b _____

c _____   d _____

e _____

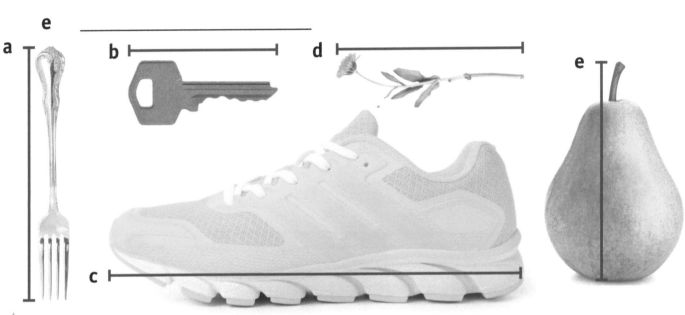

2 Measure the objects in inches.

a _____   b _____

c _____   d _____

e _____

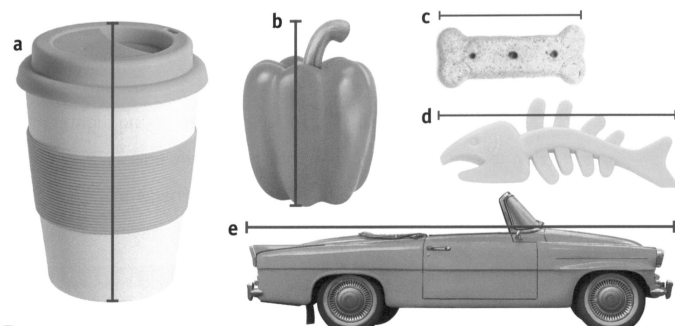

1 Use the bricks to measure the crayons.
Write the measurements in the table.

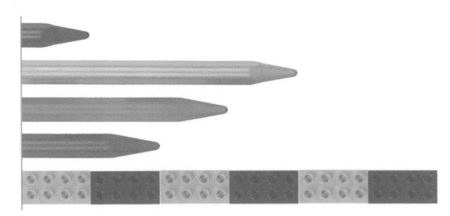

Crayon color	Length in bricks
Blue	
Green	
Red	
Pink	

2 Use the crayons above to answer the following questions.

a The blue crayon is the shortest / longest.

b The purple crayon is shorter / longer than the red crayon.

c The green crayon is the shortest / longest.

3 Order the posts from shortest to tallest.
Write the numbers 1 (shortest) to 5 (tallest) in the boxes.

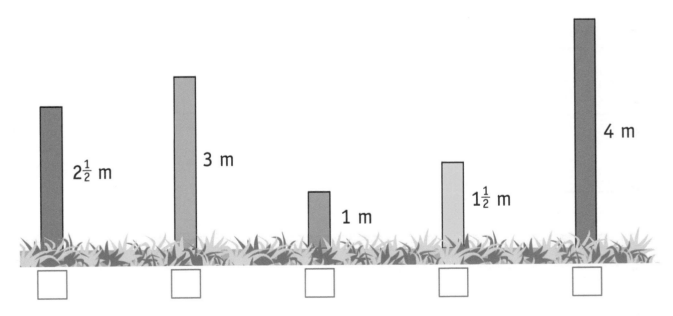

REVIEW

 Use a ruler to measure the lines in centimeters.

a _____ = ___ cm

b _____ = ___ cm

c _____ = ___ cm

d _____ = ___ cm

 Mark whether each item would be measured in feet or inches.

	Item	Feet	Inches
a	Airplane		
b	Pencil		
c	Boat		
d	Book		
e	Photo		

 Use a ruler to measure the lines in inches.

	Line	Inches
a		
b		
c		
d		

a _____ = ___ in.

b _____ = ___ in.

c _____ = ___ in.

d _____ = ___ in.

TRIANGLES

Triangles are shapes that have 3 sides and 3 angles.

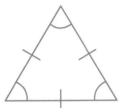

This is an equilateral triangle because all the sides are the same length and all the angles are the same size.

The marks on the sides and the angles tell you which ones are equal.

This triangle has one right angle. It is not an equilateral triangle.

This triangle has two equal sides and two equal angles. It is not an equilateral triangle.

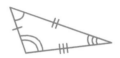

All the sides and all the angles in this triangle are different. It is not an equilateral triangle.

Examples: Use red to color the triangles that have a right angle, use blue for the ones with two equal sides and angles, and use green for the ones with all sides and angles different.

a    b 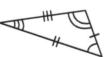   c    d

Your turn

Color all the equilateral triangles red.

   b   d   f

a    c   e   g

PRACTICE

1 Draw three different equilateral triangles.

2 Draw three triangles that each have different side lengths.

3 Draw a check mark on the equilateral triangles and an *X* on the other types of triangles.

c

f

a

d

g

b

e

h

QUADRILATERALS

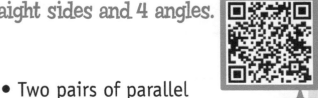

SCAN to watch video

A quadrilateral is a shape with 4 straight sides and 4 angles.

Square

- All sides equal in length
- All angles 90°
- Two pairs of parallel lines

Rectangle

- Opposite sides equal in length
- All angles 90°

Rhombus

- All sides equal in length
- Two pairs of parallel sides
- Opposite angles equal in size

Parallelogram

- Opposite sides equal in length
- Two pairs of parallel sides
- Opposite angles equal in size

Kite

- Two pairs of sides the same length
- No parallel sides

Trapezoid

- One pair of parallel sides

Examples: Color the rectangles red, rhombuses blue, kites yellow, parallelograms green, and trapezoids orange.

a   b   c   d   e

Your turn

Trace the rhombuses with red, parallelograms with purple, rectangles with pink, squares with green, trapezoids with yellow, and kites with blue.

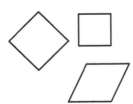

SELF CHECK Mark how you feel

Got it!	Need help...	I don't get it

Check your answers
How many did you get correct?

PRACTICE

1 Use purple to trace the parallel lines on these quadrilaterals.

  b  **d** **f**

a **c** **e** **g**

2 Draw the quadrilaterals.

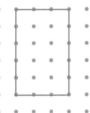 rectangle **b** square **d** rhombus

a kite **c** parallelogram **e** trapezoid

3 Use red to color the squares.

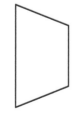 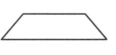 

 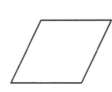 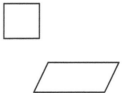

PENTAGONS AND HEXAGONS

A pentagon has 5 straight sides and 5 corners.

A hexagon has 6 straight sides and 6 corners.

Regular Pentagon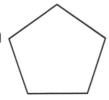

Regular Hexagon

This is an irregular pentagon.

It has 5 sides that are not the same length and 5 angles that are not equal in size.

This is an irregular hexagon.

It has 6 sides that are not the same length and 6 angles that are not equal in size.

Examples: Label the pentagons and hexagons.

a   b   c   d

__regular__   _____   _____   _____

__pentagon__   _____   _____   _____

Your turn

Trace the regular pentagons with pink, and put a red **X** on the irregular pentagons.

Trace the regular hexagons with blue, and put a red **X** on the irregular hexagons.

SELF CHECK   Mark how you feel

Got it!   Need help...   I don't get it

Check your answers
How many did you get correct?

PRACTICE

1 Trace the irregular pentagons in purple, the irregular hexagons in green, the regular pentagons in pink, and the regular hexagons in blue.

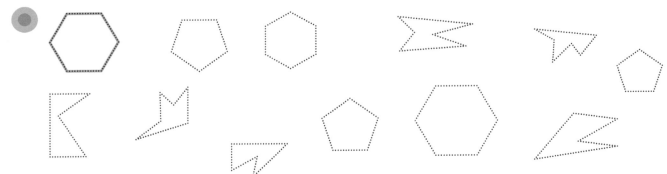

2 Draw the polygons.

Irregular hexagon   **a** Regular hexagon

b Irregular pentagon   **c** Regular pentagon

3 Fill in the table.

Shape	Regular pentagon	Irregular pentagon	Regular hexagon	Irregular hexagon
Diagram				
Number of corners				
Number of sides				

Color the equilateral triangles, and cross out other types of triangles.

   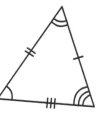   

 Color the squares, and circle the other types of quadrilaterals.

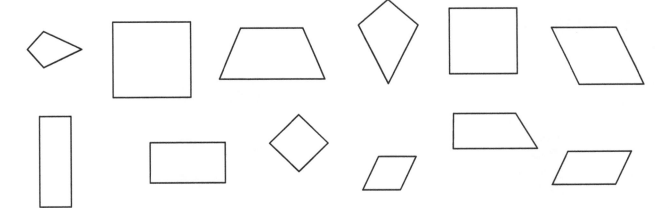

3 Complete the table.

Shape	Diagram	Number of corners	Number of sides
regular pentagon			
irregular pentagon			
regular hexagon			
irregular hexagon			

MEASURING AREA WITH UNITS

Area is how much space an object takes up. You can use the area of a smaller object to measure and compare larger areas.

It is best to use shapes that have straight sides because they do not leave spaces.

Examples: Write the missing numbers.

a

The surface of the towel has been covered with blocks.

The towel has an area of <u>30</u> blocks.

b

The surface of the book has been covered with blocks.

The book has an area of ___ blocks.

Your turn

How many blocks were used to cover the surface?

● <u>45</u> blocks cover this surface.

a ___ blocks cover this surface.

b ___ blocks cover this surface.

SELF CHECK Mark how you feel
Got it! | Need help... | I don't get it

Check your answers How many did you get correct?

PRACTICE

AREA

1 Did the shapes leave spaces when they were used to cover the surfaces? Mark the correct box.

● ✔ spaces
☐ no spaces

b ☐ spaces
☐ no spaces

d ☐ spaces
☐ no spaces

a ☐ spaces
☐ no spaces

c ☐ spaces
☐ no spaces

e ☐ spaces
☐ no spaces

 2 Jake covered the surfaces of two books with square counters.

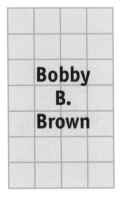

● *Garden Girl* has an area of __24__ square counters.

a *Bobby B. Brown* has an area of ____ square counters.

b _____ takes up a smaller space than _____.

c The difference in area between the two books is ____ square counters.

MEASURING AREA WITH A GRID

Grids can be used to measure area.
All the shapes in the grid must be the same shape and size.
We call each shape a *unit*.

A grid of squares

A grid of triangles

Examples: Write the missing numbers.

a This TV has an area of _12_ square units.

b This TV has an area of ____ triangle units and 4 half-triangle units.

It covers an area of ____ triangle units altogether.

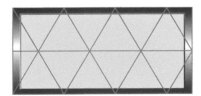

 = 1 whole ◸ = half

Your turn

Write the area.

● This TV has an area of _30_ square units.

a This book has an area of ____ square units.

SELF CHECK Mark how you feel

Got it!	Need help...	I don't get it
☺ ☐	😐 ☐	😠 ☐

Check your answers

How many did you get correct? ☐

PRACTICE

1 Write how many units were used to cover each shape.

__9__ square units

b

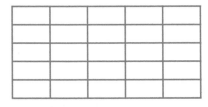

___ rectangle units

a

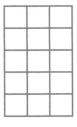

___ rectangle units

c

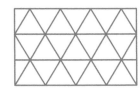

___ triangle units

___ half triangle units

total = ___ triangle units

2 Find the area of each magazine cover by counting the number of squares used to cover the surface.

 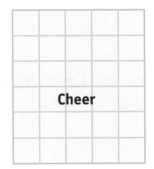 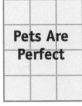

Area
= __15__ squares

Area
= ___ squares

Area
= ___ squares

Area
= ___ squares

a The magazine that covers the largest area is _____.

b The magazine that covers the smallest area is _____.

c What is the difference in area between *Cheer* and *Pets Are Perfect*? _____

d What is the difference in area between *Mountain Bikes* and *Top Travel Spots*? _____

SQUARE CENTIMETERS AND SQUARE INCHES

Square centimeters and square inches are
units of measurement.

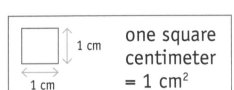 one square centimeter = 1 cm²

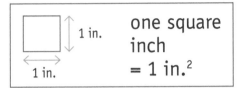 one square inch = 1 in.²

SCAN to watch video

Examples: Count the number of square centimeters
or square inches to find the area.

a Area = <u>12</u> square centimeters

= <u>12</u> cm²

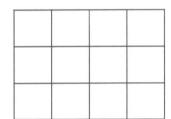

b Area = ___ square inches

= ___ in.²

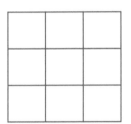

Your turn

Count the number of square centimeters or
square inches to find the area.

●

<u>4</u> square centimeters

<u>4</u> cm²

a

___ square inches

__ in.²

b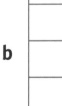

___ square centimeters

__ cm²

SELF CHECK   Mark how you feel

Got it! ☐

Need help... ☐

I don't get it ☐

Check your answers
How many did
you get correct? ☐

PRACTICE

1 Count the square centimeters to find the area of each shape. Record your answers in the table.

Shape	Area in words	Area using cm²
A	four square centimeters	4 cm²
B		
C		
D		
E		
F		

2 Use the shapes above to answer these questions.

⬤ The shape with the largest area is __B__.

a The smallest area of all the shapes is ____ cm².

b Two shapes have the same area: Shape ____ and Shape ____.

c The shape with an area of 6 square centimeters is Shape ____.

d The difference between the shape with the largest area and the shape with the smallest area is ____ cm².

e The shape with an area of 10 cm² is Shape ____.

SQUARE METERS AND SQUARE FEET

Square meters and square feet are used to measure larger areas. Square meters can be written m^2.

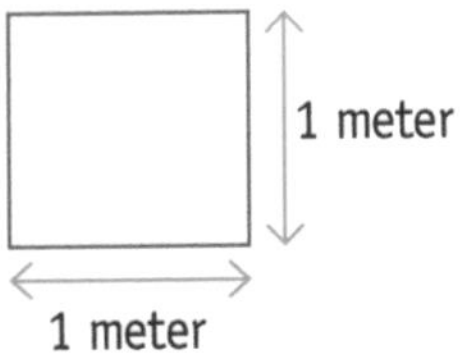

1 meter × 1 meter = 1 m^2

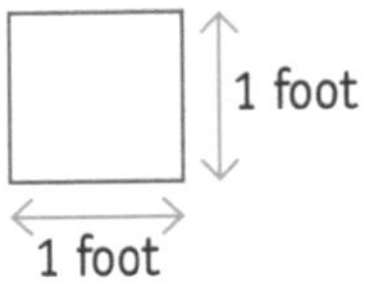

1 foot × 1 foot = 1 $ft.^2$

You would use square meters or square feet to measure the board in your classroom and your bedroom floor.

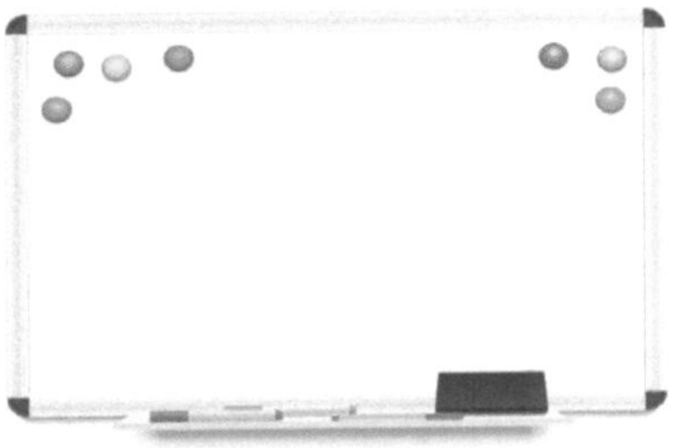

The board in your classroom

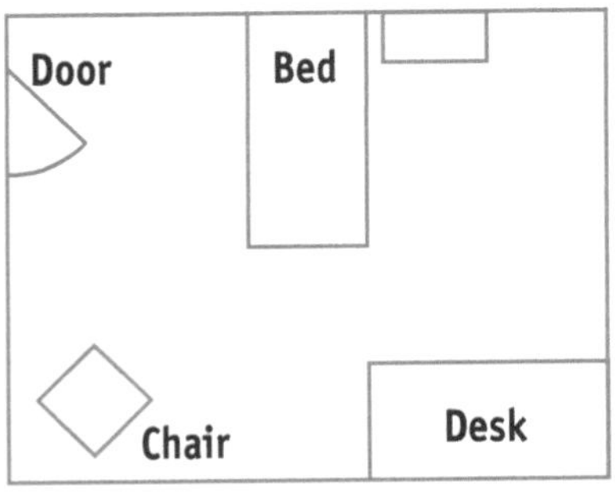

Bedroom floor

Examples: Count the square feet to find the area. □ = 1 $ft.^2$

a Area = 4 $ft.^2$

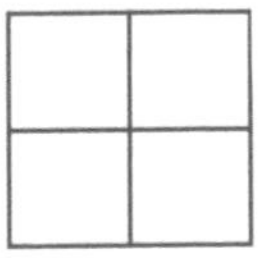

b Area = __ $ft.^2$

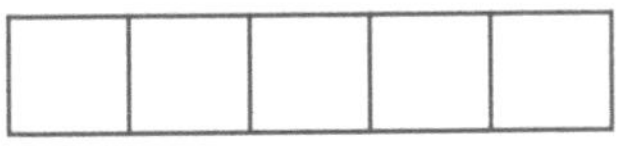

c Area = __ $ft.^2$

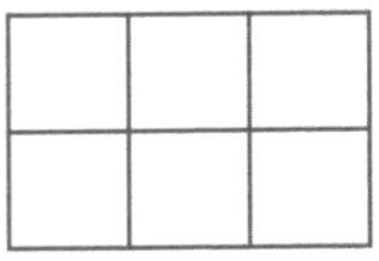

Your turn

Circle the things that would have an area less than one meter squared (1 m^2).

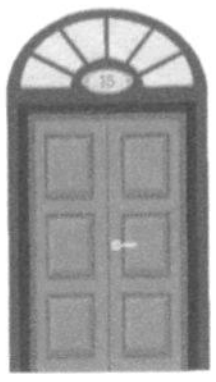

Door

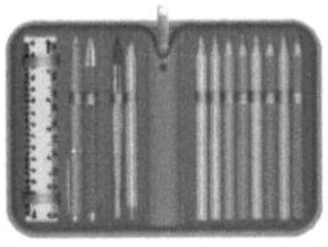

Pencil case

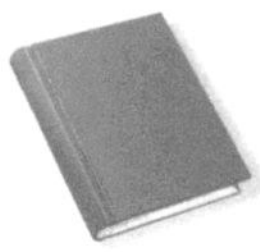

Book

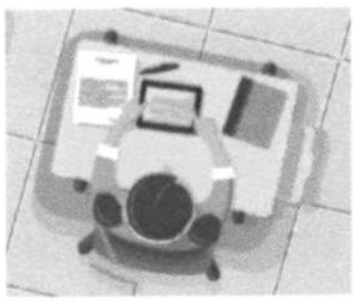

Desk top

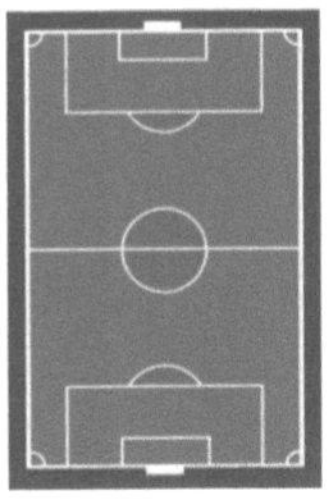

Soccer field

SELF CHECK Mark how you feel

Got it!	Need help...	I don't get it
☺ □	😐 □	☹ □

Check your answers
How many did you get correct? □

PRACTICE

1 Write the area of each shape.

a

3 feet

4 feet

Area = _____ ft.²

c

3 meters

3 meters

Area = _____ m²

b

1 meter

6 meters

Area = _____ m²

d

2 feet

4 feet

Area = _____ ft.²

2 Circle the things that would have an area of 1 square meter or more.

Magazine cover

Ruler

Sofa

Garage door

Elevator doors

Notebook

sticky note pad

3 List five things less than 1 square foot and five things more than 1 square foot.

Less than 1 sq. ft.	More than 1 sq. ft.

AREA REVIEW

 1 How many shapes cover the surface?

a ___ rectangle blocks

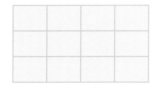

c ___ square blocks

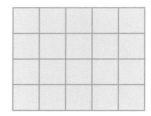

b ___ square blocks

d ___ rectangle blocks

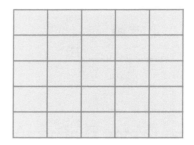

 2 Mark the shapes that are good to use to cover a surface to find its area.

a   **b**   **c**   **d**   **e**   **f**   **g**

  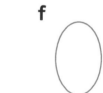

 3 Use the grids to find the areas.

a

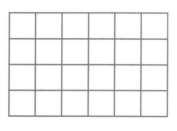

___ squares

b

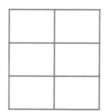

___ rectangles

c

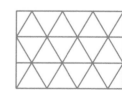

___ whole triangles

___ half triangles

Total: ___ triangles

4 Calculate the area of each shape in square centimeters or square inches.

a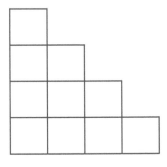

Area = ____ square centimeters

= ____ cm²

c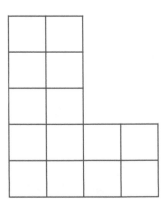

Area = ____ square centimeters

= ____ cm²

b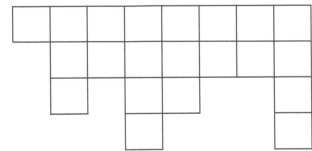

Area = ____ square inches

= ____ in².

d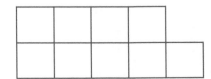

Area = ____ square inches

= ____ in².

REVIEW

5 Circle the areas that are less than 1 square foot, and cross out the areas that are larger than 1 square foot.

Bookcase

Phone

Window

Sticky note

Desk

Dollar

6 Circle the areas that are less than one square meter (1 m²), and cross out the areas larger than 1 m².

Book

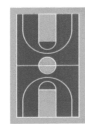

Basketball court

Plate

Door

Bowling alley

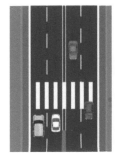

Road

7 Write the measurements using numbers and m².

a sixteen square meters = _____

b one hundred three square meters = _____

c fifty-three square meters = _____

d eighty-four square meters = _____

e forty-nine square meters = _____

f one hundred nine square meters = _____

g eight hundred twenty-six square meters = _____

h eighty-seven square meters = _____

CAPACITY

Capacity is the amount of liquid a container can hold.

The pink bucket has the largest capacity because it can hold the most liquid.

The blue bucket has the smallest capacity because it can hold the least liquid.

Glass A

Glass B

Glass B has more juice in it than Glass A.

But Glass A has a bigger capacity because it can hold more.

Examples: Draw a similar container with a smaller capacity.

a

b

c

Your turn

Circle the object with the least capacity, and cross out the object with the greatest capacity.

b

a

c

1 Circle the object with the smallest capacity.

a

b

c

2 Use these containers to answer the following questions.

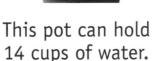

This pot can hold
14 cups of water.

This pitcher can hold
10 cups of water.

This kettle can hold
12 cups of water.

● The object with the largest capacity is the _____pot_____.

a The object with the smallest capacity is the _____.

b The difference between the objects with the
largest capacity and smallest capacity is ___ cups.

c The difference in capacity between the kettle and the pitcher
is ___ cups.

d Is the capacity of the kettle 2 cups bigger or 2 cups smaller than the
capacity of the pot? _____

COMPARING CAPACITY

The capacity of a container is the total amount it can hold when it is full.

The orange cup has only a small amount in it. But it can hold more liquid than the other cups, so it has the greatest capacity.

Examples: Number the containers to order them from least capacity (1) to greatest capacity (5).

a

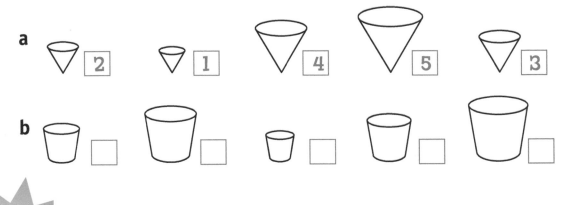

b

Your turn

Which container has the greatest capacity? Circle it.

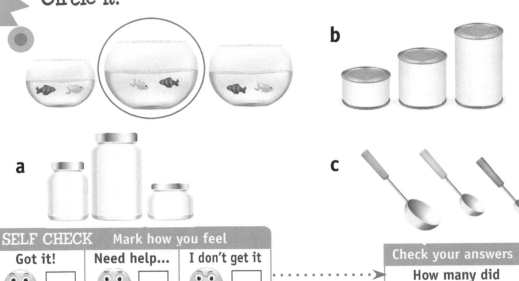

a

b

c

 PRACTICE

1 Cross out the object with the least capacity.

b

a

c

2 Which container has the larger capacity? Circle it.

d

a

e

b

f

c

g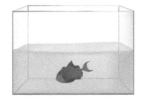

LITERS AND GALLONS

Liters and gallons are used to measure how much space a liquid takes up. The symbol for liters is L. The symbol for gallons is gal.

SCAN to watch video

This bottle of water holds one liter.
one liter = 1 L

This jug holds one gallon of milk.

one gallon = 1 gal.

Examples:

a 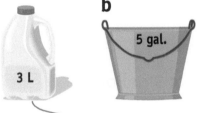 b c d

e

| 2 liters | 3 liters | 4 liters | 1 gallon | 5 gallons |

Your turn

Join the matching measurements.

⬤ 5 liters   4 L

a 12 gallons   12 gal.

b 1 liter   7 gal.

c three gallons   1 L

d seven gallons   3 gal.

e four liters   5 L

SELF CHECK   Mark how you feel

| Got it! | Need help... | I don't get it |

Check your answers
How many did you get correct?

PRACTICE

1 More or less than one liter? Circle the correct answer.

 more than / (less than) one liter

c more than / less than one liter

a more than / less than one liter

d more than / less than one liter

b more than / less than one liter

e  more than / less than one liter

2 Draw an ✗ on the things that hold less than one gallon.

b

d

a

c

e

3 Mark all the things that hold more than one gallon.

MEASURING LIQUIDS

The same amount of liquid can look different in different containers. Each mark on these pitchers shows one liter.

The juice in this pitcher measures 4 liters (4 L).

The juice in this pitcher measures 3 liters (3 L).

L is short for liters.

Examples: Color the pitchers to show 1 liter (1 L).

a    b    c    d

Your turn

What amount of juice is in each pitcher?

● __1 L__   a _____   b _____

Check your answers
How many did you get correct?

PRACTICE

1 How much liquid is in the pitchers? Match the correct label with each pitcher.

 **a** 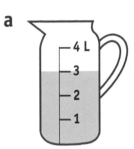 **b** 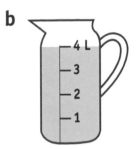 **c**

| four liters 4 L | three liters 3 L | one liter 1 L | two liters 2 L |

2 Color to show the amount in liters in each pitcher.

5 liters   **a** 6 liters   **b** 4 liters   **c** 3 liters

3 Color the smaller containers to show the amount you need to fill each large container.

 4 gal.

a   8 gal.

b   10 gal.

Circle the container in each pair with the higher capacity, and cross out the container with the lower capacity.

a

c

b

d

 Number the boxes to order the capacities of these containers from least (1) to most (5).

a

☐ ☐ ☐ ☐ ☐

b

☐ ☐ ☐ ☐ ☐

c

☐ ☐ ☐ ☐ ☐

3 Cross out the object with the least capacity, and circle the object with the most capacity in each group.

a

c

b

d

4 Write these measurements using L for liters and gal. for gallons.

a four liters = _____

d 15 gallons = _____

b 6 gallons = _____

e seven liters = _____

c twelve liters = _____

f 19 gallons = _____

5 Write "more" or "less" to describe the capacity.

a

_____ than
1 gallon

b

_____ than
1 liter

c

_____ than
1 gallon

6 Draw three things with a capacity that matches the description.

More than 1 liter	Less than 1 liter

REVIEW

7 **What amount of liquid is in each container?**

a _____

c _____

e _____

b _____

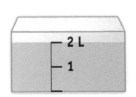

d _____

f _____

8 **Color the containers to show the amounts.**

a 1 gal.

| —10 gal. |
| —9 |
| —8 |
| —7 |
| —6 |
| —5 |
| —4 |
| —3 |
| —2 |
| —1 |

c 5 gal.

| —10 gal. |
| —9 |
| —8 |
| —7 |
| —6 |
| —5 |
| —4 |
| —3 |
| —2 |
| —1 |

e 6 gal.

| —10 gal. |
| —9 |
| —8 |
| —7 |
| —6 |
| —5 |
| —4 |
| —3 |
| —2 |
| —1 |

b 3 gal.

| —10 gal. |
| —9 |
| —8 |
| —7 |
| —6 |
| —5 |
| —4 |
| —3 |
| —2 |
| —1 |

d 7 gal.

| —10 gal. |
| —9 |
| —8 |
| —7 |
| —6 |
| —5 |
| —4 |
| —3 |
| —2 |
| —1 |

f 2 gal.

| —10 gal. |
| —9 |
| —8 |
| —7 |
| —6 |
| —5 |
| —4 |
| —3 |
| —2 |
| —1 |

MASS

Mass is how heavy something is. We use scales to measure mass.

 The empty bowl is lighter than the bowl of apples.

  The bag with 7 marbles is heavier than the bag with 2 marbles.

Examples: Circle the correct words.

a  The banana is heavier than / lighter than /(the same mass as) the apple.

b  The basketball is heavier than / lighter than / the same mass as the bowling ball.

c  The cherries are heavier than / lighter than / the same mass as the grapes.

Your turn

Circle the heavier thing in each pair.

 a  b  c

SELF CHECK Mark how you feel

Got it! ☐   Need help... ☐   I don't get it ☐

Check your answers
How many did you get correct?

PRACTICE

1 Draw an ✗ on the lighter object.

   **b**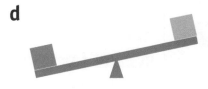

a    **c**   **e**

2 Mark the seesaws where the objects are balanced (weigh the same).

   **b**    **d**

a   **c**   **e**

3 Cross out the incorrect words.

 Abby is heavier than / ~~lighter than~~ / ~~the same mass as~~ Lin.

a  Ravi is heavier than / lighter than / the same mass as Joe.

b  Kala is heavier than / lighter than / the same mass as Ray.

c  Kim is heavier than / lighter than / the same mass as Nia.

d  Zeb is heavier than / lighter than / the same mass as Kai.

© Shell Education   146434—Catch-Up Math   **211**

KILOGRAMS AND POUNDS

A kilogram is a unit used for measuring mass. The symbol for kilogram is kg.
These items weigh about 1 kg.

A pound is another unit used for measuring mass. Two pounds are about the same as one kilogram. The symbol for pound is lb.
These items weigh about 1 lb.

SCAN to watch video

Examples: Circle the items that would be best measured in kilograms or pounds.

Your turn

Mark the items that we buy in pounds.

- ☑ potatoes
- a ☐ milk
- b ☐ apples
- c ☐ sugar
- d ☐ clothes
- e ☐ books
- f ☐ bag of chips
- g ☐ flour

SELF CHECK Mark how you feel

Got it!	Need help...	I don't get it
☐	☐	☐

Check your answers
How many did you get correct?

PRACTICE

1 Color the weights to show these masses.

●	28 kilograms	10 kg	10 kg	10 kg	5 kg	5 kg	5 kg	1 kg	1 kg	1 kg
		10 kg	10 kg	10 kg	5 kg	5 kg	5 kg	1 kg	1 kg	1 kg
a	47 pounds	10 lbs.	10 lbs.	10 lbs.	5 lbs.	5 lbs.	5 lbs.	1 lb.	1 lb.	1 lb.
		10 lbs.	10 lbs.	10 lbs.	5 lbs.	5 lbs.	5 lbs.	1 lb.	1 lb.	1 lb.
b	39 kilograms	10 kg	10 kg	10 kg	5 kg	5 kg	5 kg	1 kg	1 kg	1 kg
		10 kg	10 kg	10 kg	5 kg	5 kg	5 kg	1 kg	1 kg	1 kg
c	56 pounds	10 lbs.	10 lbs.	10 lbs.	5 lbs.	5 lbs.	5 lbs.	1 lb.	1 lb.	1 lb.
		10 lbs.	10 lbs.	10 lbs.	5 lbs.	5 lbs.	5 lbs.	1 lb.	1 lb.	1 lb.
d	69 kilograms	10 kg	10 kg	10 kg	5 kg	5 kg	5 kg	1 kg	1 kg	1 kg
		10 kg	10 kg	10 kg	5 kg	5 kg	5 kg	1 kg	1 kg	1 kg

2 What mass has been colored?

●	_49_ pounds	10 lbs.	10 lbs.	10 lbs.	5 lbs.	5 lbs.	5 lbs.	1 lb.	1 lb.	1 lb.
		10 lbs.	10 lbs.	10 lbs.	5 lbs.	5 lbs.	5 lbs.	1 lb.	1 lb.	1 lb.
a	___ kilograms	10 kg	10 kg	10 kg	5 kg	5 kg	5 kg	1 kg	1 kg	1 kg
		10 kg	10 kg	10 kg	5 kg	5 kg	5 kg	1 kg	1 kg	1 kg
b	___ pounds	10 lbs.	10 lbs.	10 lbs.	5 lbs.	5 lbs.	5 lbs.	1 lb.	1 lb.	1 lb.
		10 lbs.	10 lbs.	10 lbs.	5 lbs.	5 lbs.	5 lbs.	1 lb.	1 lb.	1 lb.
c	___ kilograms	10 kg	10 kg	10 kg	5 kg	5 kg	5 kg	1 kg	1 kg	1 kg
		10 kg	10 kg	10 kg	5 kg	5 kg	5 kg	1 kg	1 kg	1 kg
d	___ pounds	10 lbs.	10 lbs.	10 lbs.	5 lbs.	5 lbs.	5 lbs.	1 lb.	1 lb.	1 lb.
		10 lbs.	10 lbs.	10 lbs.	5 lbs.	5 lbs.	5 lbs.	1 lb.	1 lb.	1 lb.

3 Write the masses in short form.

● 8 kilograms _8 kg_

● 12 pounds _12 lbs._

a seven kilograms _____

d thirty-two pounds _____

b nine pounds _____

e twenty-eight kilograms _____

c 24 kilograms _____

f 43 pounds _____

4 Use Mya's shopping to answer the following questions.

| Bananas 3 kg | Pineapple 1 kg | Oranges 2 kg | Apples 2 kg | Grapes 2 kg |

● What is the mass of the oranges? _2 kg_

a The pineapple has a mass of _____.

b The apples and grapes together have a mass of _____.

c The total mass of Mya's shopping is _____.

d The heaviest item is the _____.

e Which three items have the same mass?

_____, _____, and _____

f What is the difference in mass between the bananas and the pineapple? _____

g What is the lightest item? _____

5 Guy bought 2 bags of rice, 1 package of fish, 1 package of steak, and 3 bags of apples.

| Rice 1 lb. | Fish 3 lbs. | Steak 1 lb. | Apples 2 lbs. |

⬤ What is the mass of the rice Guy bought? __2 lbs.__

a How much does Guy's shopping weigh altogether? _____

b How much do the fish and the steak weigh? _____

c What two items have the same mass?

_____ and _____

d How much do the two bags of rice weigh? _____

e What weighs more: the fish or the 3 bags of apples?

_____

 6 Circle the item that could be getting weighed.

2 kg

• a chicken

• a loaf of bread

b **3 kg**

• a bag of potatoes

• a pencil case

a **1 lb.**

• a grape

• a bag of flour

c **8 lbs.**

• a can of beans

• a watermelon

COMPARING AND ORDERING MASS

We need to compare the masses of items before we can arrange them in order of mass. We work out which item is lightest and which item is heaviest.

SCAN to watch video

Crow 5 kg   Lucky 4 kg   Scratcher 3 kg

Scratcher is the lightest chicken. The heaviest chicken is Crow.

Examples: Draw more objects so the group is heavier.

	a	b	c
Lighter			
Heavier			

Your turn

Order these objects from lightest (1) to heaviest (3).

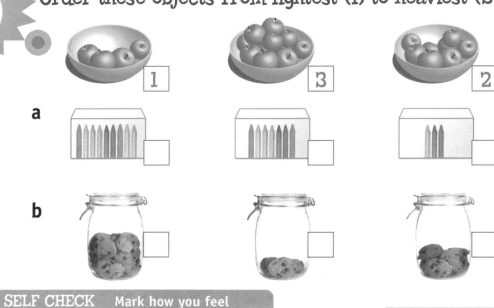

1   3   2

a

b

SELF CHECK   Mark how you feel

Got it!   Need help...   I don't get it

Check your answers
How many did you get correct?

© Shell Education

PRACTICE

1 Ben used the balance scales to measure these items.

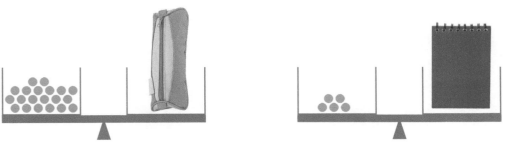

⦿ The heaviest object is the <u>pencil case</u> .

a The lightest object is the _____.

b ___ marbles balanced the pencil case.

c The calculator is balanced with ___ marbles.

d Does the glue stick weigh more or less than the notebook? _____

e Does the calculator weigh more or less than the glue stick? _____

f If Ben places the notebook and glue stick on one side of the scale, how many marbles does he need to balance them?

_____ marbles

g If Ben places all the objects on one side of the scale, how many marbles does he need to balance them?

_____ marbles

MASS REVIEW

1 Circle the lighter item in each pair.

a

c

b

d

2 Draw an ✘ on the lighter objects, draw a check mark on the heavier objects, and circle the objects that weigh the same.

a

c

e

b

d

f

3 Circle the correct words.

a

The brown box is heavier than / lighter than / the same mass as the pink box.

b

The blue box is heavier than / lighter than / the same mass as the green box.

c

The purple box is heavier than / lighter than / the same mass as the red box.

REVIEW

 4 Order these items from heaviest (1) to lightest (5).

a

 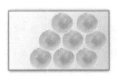 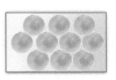  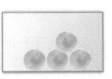

☐ ☐ ☐ ☐ ☐

b

☐ ☐ ☐ ☐ ☐

c

☐ ☐ ☐ ☐ ☐

 5 Ali used the balance scales to measure these items.

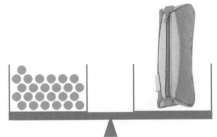 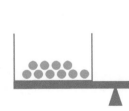  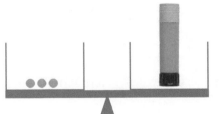

a The lightest item is the _____.

b The heaviest item is the _____.

c ___ marbles balance the glue stick.

d Is the stapler lighter or heavier than the glue stick?

e If Ali placed the glue stick and the stapler on one side of the scale, how many marbles does he need to balance them? ___

REVIEW

6 Color the weights to show these masses.

a	17 kilograms	10 kg	10 kg	10 kg	5 kg	5 kg	5 kg	1 kg	1 kg	1 kg	
		10 kg	10 kg	10 kg	5 kg	5 kg	5 kg	1 kg	1 kg	1 kg	
b	23 pounds	10 lbs.	10 lbs.	10 lbs.	5 lbs.	5 lbs.	5 lbs.	1 lb.	1 lb.	1 lb.	
		10 lbs.	10 lbs.	10 lbs.	5 lbs.	5 lbs.	5 lbs.	1 lb.	1 lb.	1 lb.	
c	52 kilograms	10 kg	10 kg	10 kg	5 kg	5 kg	5 kg	1 kg	1 kg	1 kg	
		10 kg	10 kg	10 kg	5 kg	5 kg	5 kg	1 kg	1 kg	1 kg	
d	49 pounds	10 lbs.	10 lbs.	10 lbs.	5 lbs.	5 lbs.	5 lbs.	1 lb.	1 lb.	1 lb.	
		10 lbs.	10 lbs.	10 lbs.	5 lbs.	5 lbs.	5 lbs.	1 lb.	1 lb.	1 lb.	

7 What mass has been colored?

a	____ pounds	10 lbs.	10 lbs.	10 lbs.	5 lbs.	5 lbs.	5 lbs.	1 lb.	1 lb.	1 lb.	
		10 lbs.	10 lbs.	10 lbs.	5 lbs.	5 lbs.	5 lbs.	1 lb.	1 lb.	1 lb.	
b	____ kilograms	10 kg	10 kg	10 kg	5 kg	5 kg	5 kg	1 kg	1 kg	1 kg	
		10 kg	10 kg	10 kg	5 kg	5 kg	5 kg	1 kg	1 kg	1 kg	
c	____ pounds	10 lbs.	10 lbs.	10 lbs.	5 lbs.	5 lbs.	5 lbs.	1 lb.	1 lb.	1 lb.	
		10 lbs.	10 lbs.	10 lbs.	5 lbs.	5 lbs.	5 lbs.	1 lb.	1 lb.	1 lb.	
d	____ kilograms	10 kg	10 kg	10 kg	5 kg	5 kg	5 kg	1 kg	1 kg	1 kg	
		10 kg	10 kg	10 kg	5 kg	5 kg	5 kg	1 kg	1 kg	1 kg	

REVIEW

 8 Write the masses in words.

a 22 lbs. _____

b 43 kg _____

c 7 lbs. _____

d 84 kg _____

e 21 lbs. _____

 9 Circle the item that could be getting weighed.

a **10 lbs.**

- bag of potatoes
- an apple

b **1 kg**

- bag of carrots
- a cherry

c **5 lbs.**

- loaf of bread
- bag of rice

ANALOG CLOCKS—O'CLOCK AND 30

Analog clocks are divided into 12 parts. Each part is equal to one hour passing.

This time can be written as 5 o'clock or 5:00.

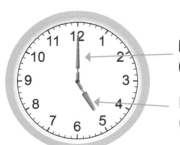

Minute hand (big hand)

Hour hand (little hand)

SCAN to watch video

Examples: Fill in the blanks, and write the time.

a

The minute hand (__big__ hand) points to the _12_.

The hour hand (__little__ hand) points to the _3_.

The time is ___3 o'clock___.

It can also be written as 3:00.

b

The minute hand (__big__ hand) points to the _6_.

The hour hand (__little__ hand) is between the _7_ and _8_.

The time is ___7:30___.

c

The minute hand (_____ hand) points to the ___.

The hour hand (_____ hand) points to the ___.

The time is _____.

Your turn

What is the time on each analog clock?

___9:30___

a _____

b _____

SELF CHECK Mark how you feel

Got it! ☐

Need help... ☐

I don't get it ☐

Check your answers
How many did you get correct?

© Shell Education

PRACTICE

1 Write the time shown on each clock.

⬤ _____6:30_____

b _____

d _____

a _____

c _____

e _____

2 Draw hands on the clocks to show the time.

⬤ 10 o'clock

c 5:00

f 7:30

a 12:30

d 1:30

g 1:00

b 8:30

e 11 o'clock

h 2:30

ANALOG CLOCKS—15 AND 45

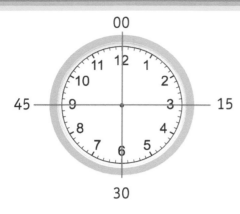

Imagine the clock has been cut into four parts, or quarters. Each quarter is 15 minutes.

15 minutes is a quarter of an hour.

Examples: Fill in the blanks.

a

The minute hand (_big_ hand) points to the _3_,
so it is _15_ minutes past the hour.
The time is _4:15_.

b

The minute hand (_big_ hand) points to the _9_,
so it is _45_ minutes past the hour.
The time is _6:45_.

c

The minute hand (_____ hand) points to the ___,
so it is ___ minutes past the hour.
The time is _____.

Your turn

What is the time on each clock?

___6:15___   **a** _____   **b** _____   **c** _____

PRACTICE

1 Join the matching times.

| 4:15 |
| 10:15 |
| 10:45 |
| 7:15 |
| 6:45 |
| 11:45 |

a

b

c

d

e

2 Draw hands on the clocks to show the time.

7:45

b 12:45

d 2:15

a 5:15

c 3:45

e 11:15

FIVE-MINUTE INTERVALS

The amount of time between two given times is called a time interval.

There are 60 minutes in one hour.

Each jump is 5 minutes.

The black numbers show what hour it is. The blue numbers show the minutes.

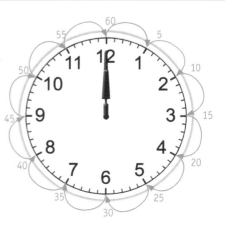

Examples: Fill in the blanks.

a

The small (hour) hand is on the 7. The big (minute) hand is on the 2. Count 5-minute intervals from 12. The time is __7:10__.

b
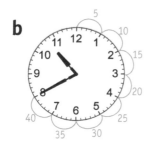
The small (hour) hand is between 10 and 11. So, the time is between 10:00 and 11:00. The big (minute) hand is on the 8. Count 5-minute intervals from 12. The time is __10:40__.

c
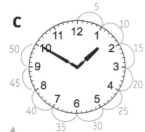
The small (hour) hand is between the ____ and ____. So, the time is between ____ and ____. The big (minute) hand is on the ____. Count 5-minute intervals from 12. The time is _____.

Your turn

Draw the jumps, and write the time.

____9:20____

a _____

b _____

PRACTICE

1 Show the times on the clocks.

● 8:20

b 9:25

d 10:40

a 6:55

c 3:45

e 11:50

2 Join the matching times.

●

c

a

6:10
3:05
1:55
6:50
12:20
9:35

d

b

e

PRACTICE

 Match each label to the correct clock.

a	b	c	d

3:15	6:40	8:50	10:25	2:55

 Write the times shown on the clocks.

 2:05   **b** _____   **d** _____   **f** _____

a _____   **c** _____   **e** _____   **g** _____

 Draw hands on the clocks to show the time.

 12:50   **a** 2:40   **b** 2:25   **c** 5:10

TIME

DIGITAL TIME

Digital clocks use numbers to show the time. They have no hands.

The numbers on this side show the hours. →  ← The numbers on this side show the minutes.

Examples: What time is it?

a
<u>1 o'clock</u>

c
_____

e
_____

b
<u>eight thirty</u>

d
_____

f
_____

Your turn

Join the matching times.

●    three fifteen

a   two o'clock

b    five thirty

c   seven thirty-five

SELF CHECK   Mark how you feel
Got it! □   Need help... □   I don't get it □

Check your answers
How many did you get correct?

© Shell Education   146434—Catch-Up Math   229

PRACTICE

 1 What time is shown on these digital clocks?

b 5:00

d 3:30

two o'clock

_____

_____

a 4:15

c 7:25

e 8:40

_____

_____

_____

2 Fill in the times on the digital clocks.

7:00

b [:]

d [:]

seven o'clock

eleven twenty

nine fifty-five

a [:]

c [:]

e [:]

eight thirty

twelve o'clock

six forty-five

3 Join the matching times.

 10:30

one forty

ten thirty

a 1:40

nine o'clock

b 9:00

twelve fifteen

c 11:10

eleven ten

d 12:15

1 Write the time shown on each analog clock.

a _____

d _____

g _____

b _____

e _____

h _____

c _____

f _____

i _____

REVIEW

 2 Match each label with the correct analog clock.

a    b    c    d    e

2:10		5:50		11:35

11:05		2:20

 3 What is the time on each digital clock?

a

_____

c

_____

e

_____

b

_____

d

_____

f

_____

ANSWERS

1. WHOLE NUMBERS

Whole Numbers

Page 9 – Example(s)

Example 2: 47 or 74

Page 9 – Your Turn

Red: 0, 4, 7, 8, 5, 6, 9   Blue: 62, 28, 43, 37, 99, 17, 74, 89

Page 10 – Practice

1

1	2	3	4	5	6	7	8	9	10
11	12	13	14	15	16	17	18	19	20
21	22	23	24	25	26	27	28	29	30
31	32	33	34	35	36	37	38	39	40
41	42	43	44	45	46	47	48	49	50
51	52	53	54	55	56	57	58	59	60
61	62	63	64	65	66	67	68	69	70
71	72	73	74	75	76	77	78	79	80
81	82	83	84	85	86	87	88	89	90
91	92	93	94	95	96	97	98	99	100

2 a 53   c 46   e 41   g 86
  b 36   d 85   f 16   h 31

3 a
  20 21   25   29   34   38 40

  b
  50 52   57   60   63   69 70

  c
  80 81   85 87 89   93   100

4 a 48   b 59   c 64

5 a 26   d 56   g 71
  b 35   e 32   h 47
  c 21   f 80   i 90

6 a 45   c 32   e 38   g 80   i 97
  b 30   d 59   f 85   h 44

Tens and Ones

Page 13 – Example(s)

Example 2: 8 tens

Page 13 – Your Turn

	Number	Tens	Ones	Base 10
a	38	3	8	
b	26	2	6	

Page 14 – Practice

1

	Number	Tens	Ones
a	56		
b	24		
c	83		
d	97		
e	68		

2 a 45 = 4 tens and 5 ones
       = 40 + 5
       = 45

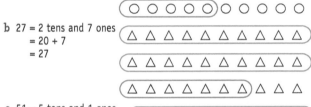

  b 27 = 2 tens and 7 ones
       = 20 + 7
       = 27

  c 51 = 5 tens and 1 ones
       = 50 + 1
       = 51

  d 18 = 1 tens and 8 ones
       = 10 + 8
       = 18

Expanded Numbers

Page 16 – Example(s)

Example 2: 10 + 10 + 10 + 10
1 + 1 + 1 + 1 + 1 + 1 + 1
40
7
10 + 7 = 47

Page 16 – Your Turn

	Number	Base 10	Expanded Form
a	16		10 + 6
b	52		50 + 2
c	67		60 + 7
d	73		70 + 3

Page 17 – Practice

1 a 20 + 7   c 30 + 1   e 60 + 3   g 90 + 8   i 60 + 0
  b 50 + 9   d 40 + 4   f 10 + 9   h 80 + 4

2

	Number	Base 10 Tens	Base 10 Ones	Expanded Form
a	72	▯▯▯▯▯▯▯	▯▯	70 + 2
b	97	▯▯▯▯▯▯▯▯▯	▯▯▯▯▯▯▯	90 + 7
c	34	▯▯▯	▯▯▯▯	30 + 4
d	85	▯▯▯▯▯▯▯▯	▯▯▯▯▯	80 + 5
e	13	▯	▯▯▯	10 + 3
f	49	▯▯▯▯	▯▯▯▯▯▯▯▯▯	40 + 9
g	28	▯▯	▯▯▯▯▯▯▯▯	20 + 8

3 a 49   c 77   e 26
  b 54   d 98

4 a   c   e

  b   d

Counting by Tens

Page 19 – Example(s)

Example 2: 88, 78, 68, 58

Page 19 – Your Turn

  a 60, 50, 40   b 33, 43, 53   c 47, 37, 27

Page 20 – Practice

1 a 79, 69, 49   c 30, 50, 60, 80, 90   d 57, 67, 87, 97
  b 44, 54   e 78, 88, 98

2 a 87, 67, 37, 17   e 22, 32, 62, 72, 82
  b 38, 58, 88, 98   f 83, 73, 63, 43, 33, 23
  c 21, 41, 51, 71   g 94, 64, 54, 34
  d 30, 50, 60, 70, 90

Odd and Even Numbers

Page 21 – Example(s)

Example 2: odd, odd

Page 21 – Your Turn

Red: 25, 39, 93, 57, 81   Blue: 72, 48, 40, 16, 90

Page 22 – Practice

1 a 4, 6, 8 or 0   b 3, 5, 7 or 9
2 a Choose from 12, 14, 16, 18, 20, 22, 24, 26, 28
  b Choose from 52, 54, 56, 58, 60, 62, 64, 66, 68
  c Choose from 82, 84, 86, 88, 90, 92, 94, 96, 98
  d Choose from 2, 4, 6, 8, 10, 12, 14, 16, 18

3 a Choose from 71, 73, 75, 77, 79, 81, 83, 85, 87, 89
  b Choose from 1, 3, 5, 7, 9, 11, 13, 15, 17, 19
  c Choose from 51, 53, 55, 57, 59, 61, 63
  d Choose from 21, 23, 25, 27, 29, 31, 33, 35, 37, 39, 41, 43

4 a 56, 58, 60   d 46, 48, 50   g 69, 67, 65
  b 87, 89, 91   e 8, 6, 4   h 86, 84, 82
  c 95, 97, 99   f 20, 18, 16   i 37, 35, 33

Counting by Twos

Page 23 – Example(s)

Example 3: 28, 30. 32, 37, 39, 41

Page 23 – Your Turn

  a 51, 53, 55, 57, 59   c 41, 43, 45, 47, 49
  b 86, 88, 90, 92, 94   d 63, 65, 67, 69, 71

Page 24 – Practice

1 a 76, 74, 68, 66, 62, 60   c 34, 36, 40, 42, 44, 48, 50, 52
  b 89, 87, 83, 77, 75, 73   d 76, 78, 80, 86, 88, 92, 94

2	4	6	8	10
12	14	16	18	20
22	24	26	28	30
32	34	36	38	40
42	44	46	48	50
52	54	56	58	60
62	64	66	68	70
72	74	76	78	80
82	84	86	88	90
92	94	96	98	100
Even numbers				

1	3	5	7	9
11	13	15	17	19
21	23	25	27	29
31	33	35	37	39
41	43	45	47	49
51	53	55	57	59
61	63	65	67	69
71	73	75	77	79
81	83	85	87	89
91	93	95	97	99
Odd numbers				

Counting by Fives

Page 25 – Example(s)

Example 3: 25, 30, 35, 40
Example 4: 55, 50, 45, 40

Page 25 – Your Turn

  a 15, 20   c 60, 55   e 5, 0
  b 50, 55   d 50, 45   f 55, 60

Page 26 – Practice

1 a 40, 50, 55   c 95, 85, 80   e 80, 65
  b 50, 40, 35   d 60, 55   f 35, 30

2 a 20, 10, 0   b 60, 65, 75   c 45, 35, 25

3	1	2	3	4	5	6	7	8	9	10
	11	12	13	14	15	16	17	18	19	20
	21	22	23	24	25	26	27	28	29	30
	31	32	33	34	35	36	37	38	39	40
	41	42	43	44	45	46	47	48	49	50
	51	52	53	54	55	56	57	58	59	60
	61	62	63	64	65	66	67	68	69	70
	71	72	73	74	75	76	77	78	79	80
	81	82	83	84	85	86	87	88	89	90
	91	92	93	94	95	96	97	98	99	100

Patterns

Page 27 – Example(s)

16, 15
The pattern is to subtract 1.

19, 18, 17, 16, 15

Page 27 – Your Turn

a 75, 74, 73   Rule – 1
b 35, 40, 45   Rule + 5
c 48, 50, 52   Rule + 2
d 19, 21, 23   Rule + 2

Page 28 – Practice

1 a 60, 55, 50   Rule – 5
   b 80, 90, 100   Rule + 10
   c 33, 35, 37   Rule + 2
   d 8, 10, 12   Rule + 2
   e 91, 90, 89   Rule – 1

2 a 64   c 38   e 86
   b 38   d 58   f 65

3 a 12, 20, 28, 32   b 28, 31, 40, 43   c 35, 40, 55, 60

Hundreds

Page 29 – Example(s)

Example 2: 300, 200, 100

Page 29 – Your Turn

1 127, 328, 425, 408
2 a 200, 300, 500   b 700, 600, 400

Page 30 – Practice

1 a [ ][ ][ ][ ][ ][ ][ ][ ] 800
   b [ ][ ][ ][ ][ ] 500
   c [ ][ ] 200
   d [ ][ ][ ][ ][ ][ ][ ] 700

2 a 600, 400, 300   d 500, 300
   b 800, 600, 500   e 200, 300, 500
   c 700, 900

3 a 100   b 800   c 900

Modeling Hundreds

Page 31 – Example(s)

Page 31 – Your Turn

1 a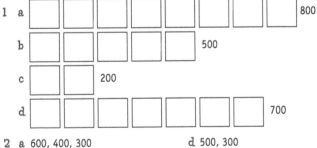
2 a 674   b 227

Page 32 – Practice

1 a 2 hundreds, 1 ten, 3 ones = 213
   b 1 hundreds, 3 tens, 4 ones = 134
   c 5 hundreds, 0 tens, 6 ones = 506
   d 8 hundreds, 4 tens, 0 ones = 840
   e 6 hundreds, 5 tens, 2 ones = 652

2 a 360   b 509   c 761

Ordering Three-Digit Numbers

Page 33 – Your Turn

1 a 903, 910, 924, 951   c 127, 240, 316, 903
   b 124, 302, 417, 425

2 a 918, 411, 215, 116   c 210, 201, 120, 102
   b 712, 545, 317, 103

Page 34 – Practice

1 a 240, 245, 249   c 103, 130, 301
   b 425, 427, 472   d 603, 613, 630

2 a 749, 711, 703   c 219, 211, 129
   b 143, 140, 104   d 613, 316, 136

3 a 217, 418, 479, 987   b 242, 656, 848, 979

4 a 4, 1, 3, 2   c 1, 2, 3, 4
   b 3, 2, 4, 1

Smallest and Largest Three-Digit Numbers

Page 35 – Your Turn

a 789   b 129   c 104   d 379

Page 36 – Practice

1 a 971   d 876   g 871   j 431
   b 864   e 321   h 610   k 943
   c 984   f 953   i 630   l 774

2 a 542 245   d 975 579
   b 389 983   e 246 642
   c 406 640   f 831 138

ANSWERS

3

	Largest number	Smallest number
a	971	179
b	540	405
c	862	268
d	943	349
e	874	478

Place Value to 100

Page 37 – Example(s)

Example 3: 5 tens and 3 ones

Page 37 – Your Turn

(29) (93) (43) (72) (17) (85) (35) (11) (33)

(57) (79) (94) (48) (20) (62) (81) (99) (40)

Page 38 – Practice

1 a 41   c 87   e 75   g 39
   b 36   d 14   f 88   h 23

2 a forty   b eighty-five   c ninety-three

3 a 6(8)   b 9(0)   c 4(4)   d 1(7)

4 a 4   b 8   c 4   d 9

5 a ones   c ones   e tens   g ones   i ones
   b ones   d tens   f ones   h tens

Number Expanders for Three-Digit Numbers

Page 39 – Your Turn

a

1	hundreds	3	tens	5	ones

1	3	tens	5	ones

1	3	5	ones

Page 40 – Practice

1 a 3 hundreds, 4 tens, 2 ones
   34 tens, 2 ones
   342 ones

   b 5 hundreds, 6 tens, 0 ones
   56 tens, 0 ones
   560 ones

2 a 249   b 347   c 981

3 a 72 tens, 3 ones   c 178 ones
   b 6 hundreds, 4 tens, 3 ones

Values

Page 41 – Example(s)

Example 2: (from left to right) 100, 70, 8

Page 41 – Your Turn

(7)(7)7   (4)1(6)   (9)0(9)

(1)(4)0   (1)0(2)   (8)4(9)

(7)(3)8   (6)2(5)   (1)8(6)   (2)3(6)

Page 42 – Practice

1 a 278   b 643   c 851   d 427

2 63(4)   87(4)

3 4(8)3   5(8)1   3(8)2

4 (5)25 (5)99 (5)77 (5)01 (5)82 (5)45

5 Sample answers:
   a 791, 725, 704, 782, 719   c 30, 439, 637, 39, 931
   b 4, 24, 94, 834, 114

Greater Than, Less Than, Equal To

Page 43 – Example(s)

Example 3: <, no, no, yes

Page 43 – Your Turn

a True   b True   c True   d True   e False

Page 44 – Practice

1 a <   c >   e =
   b <   d <   f >

2 a is less than   d is greater than
   b is less than   e is equal to
   c is greater than   f is equal to

3 a 1, 21   d 101, 123   g 451, 451
   b 52, 53   e 137, 137
   c 44, 31   f 627, 682

Three-Digit Numbers

Page 45 – Example(s)

Example 2: six hundred thirty four

Page 45 – Your Turn

a two hundred forty-eight   b nine hundred fifty-two

Page 46 – Practice

1 a 246   c 450   e 916   g 777
   b 802   d 380   f 691   h 508

2 a two hundred seventy   f nine hundred ninety-nine
   b three hundred thirteen   g eight hundred forty
   c nine hundred nine   h five hundred eleven
   d eight hundred twenty-one   i six hundred ninety-six
   e one hundred seventeen

Rounding to the Nearest Ten

Page 47 – Example(s)

Example 2: 40

Page 47 – Your Turn

a 30   b 80   c 90

Page 48 – Practice

1 a 60   c 20   e 40   g 70
   b 70   d 100   f 30   h 60

2 a 360   c 120   e 230   g 620
   b 140   d 440   f 590   h 760

3 a 610   b 970   c 840   d 360

Four-Digit Numbers

Page 49 – Example(s)

Example 2:

  b 4 thousands, 0 hundreds, 3 tens, 2 ones

  c five thousand nine hundred three

Page 49 – Your Turn

  a three thousand, four hundred ninety-two

  b six thousand fifty-seven

Page 50 – Practice

1 a 6,219   b 3,711   c 8,216   d 9,537

2 a two thousand, four hundred sixty-two

  b four thousand, four hundred ninety-one

  c nine thousand, three hundred seventy-nine

3 a 1,392; 2,468; 7,110; 8,743   c 8,219; 8,921; 9,099; 9,990

  b 2,498; 3,470; 3,740; 5,476

4 a 8,932; 6,419; 2,495; 1,249   c 8,211; 8,121; 2,181; 1,128

  b 7,116; 6,117; 1,716; 1,176

Place Value to 1,000

Page 51 – Example(s)

Example 3: 6 hundreds, 2 tens, and 1 ones

Page 51 – Your Turn

7(1)3   3(0)2   9(3)1   2(4)1

2(2)9   8(5)0   (1)70

4(3)6   5(1)9   3(5)2

Page 52 – Practice

1 a 134   b 360   c 507

2

	Number	Hundreds	Tens	Ones
a	231	2	3	1
b	859	8	5	9
c	714	7	1	4
d	902	9	0	2
e	530	5	3	0

3 4 tens: 740, 349, 540

  2 hundreds: 251, 298, 293

  7 ones: 777, 817, 417

4 a ones   d tens   g hundreds

  b hundreds   e ones

  c ones   f tens

Place Value and Four-Digit Numbers

Page 53 – Example(s)

Example 3

Thousands	Hundreds	Tens	Ones
4	2	7	3

Page 53 – Your Turn

6(9)69   9,2(0)3   7,3(1)2   4,8(1)1

2,8(1)2   4,1(5)9   5,7(0)2   3,7(8)9   7,0(0)2

Page 54 – Practice

1

	Number	Thousands	Hundreds	Tens	Ones
a	6,137	6	1	3	7
b	8,451	8	4	5	1
c	1,459	1	4	5	9
d	5,458	5	4	5	8
e	2,104	2	1	0	4
f	7,002	7	0	0	2

2 a 3,617   b 4,258   c 5,638   d 6,941

3 2 ones (red): 1,422; 8,242; 4,812

  7 tens (blue): 5,471; 3,878; 2,573; 3,470; 1,070

  9 hundreds (green): 4,963; 3,913; 5,945

  6 thousands (purple): 6,423; 6,735

Expanded Form of Four-Digit Numbers

Page 55 – Your Turn

1 (base-10 blocks figure)

2 1,000 + 400 + 30 + 2

Page 56 – Practice

1

Number	Base 10	Abacus	Expanded Form
a 3,495			3,000 + 400 + 90 + 5
b 4,321			4,000 + 300 + 20 + 1
c 2,534			2,000 + 500 + 30 + 4
d 7,103			7,000 + 100 + 3

2 a 4,000 + 700 + 10 + 6   e 5,000 + 200 + 70 + 1

  b 9,000 + 200 + 10 + 9   f 1,000 + 300 + 90 + 4

  c 3,000 + 200 + 3   g 7,000 + 500 + 30 + 6

  d 6,000 + 100 + 80   h 8,000 + 600 + 20 + 5

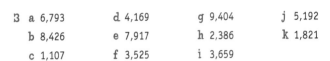

3 a 6,793   d 4,169   g 9,404   j 5,192
   b 8,426   e 7,917   h 2,386   k 1,821
   c 1,107   f 3,525   i 3,659

Modeling Four-Digit Numbers

Page 58 – Example(s)

Example 3: 1,568

Page 58 – Your Turn

   a 2,412   b 3,144

Page 59 – Practice

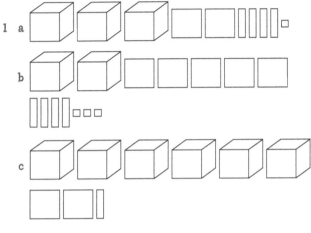

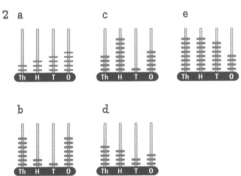

Rounding

Page 60 – Example(s)

Example 3: 4,000

Page 60 – Your Turn

1   40   3   300   5   2,000
2   120   4   1,300

Page 61 – Practice

1 a 10   c 30   e 380   g 1,250
   b 30   d 480   f 280   h 3,280

2 a 500   c 400   e 6,200   g 1,700
   b 500   d 9,900   f 4,100   h 9,700

3 a 3,000   c 10,000   e 2,000
   b 6,000   d 7,000

4 a 5,470   b 5,500   c 5,000

Whole Number Review Page 62

1 Red: 2, 1, 5, 4
   Blue: 47, 13, 26, 38, 69
   Green: 457, 506, 747, 711, 123
   Purple: 6,328, 3,206, 8,258, 4,007, 4,151, 1,289

2 a 22   d 425   g 1,808
   b 36   e 2,305   h 4,727
   c 350   f 4,119

3 a 17   d 186   g 1,837
   b 30   e 291   h 3,594
   c 214   f 1,383

4

	Number	Thousands	Hundreds	Tens	Ones
a	39	0	0	3	9
b	85	0	0	8	5
c	76	0	0	7	6
d	204	0	2	0	4
e	193	0	1	9	3
f	784	0	7	8	4
g	830	0	8	3	0
h	4,158	4	1	5	8
i	6,007	6	0	0	7
j	8,403	8	4	0	3
k	9,093	9	0	9	3

5 a 10 + 5   e 400 + 90
   b 20 + 2   f 2,000 + 500 + 90 + 3
   c 100 + 80 + 1   g 3,000 + 800 + 40 + 9
   d 200 + 50 + 6   h 6,000 + 400 + 50 + 2

6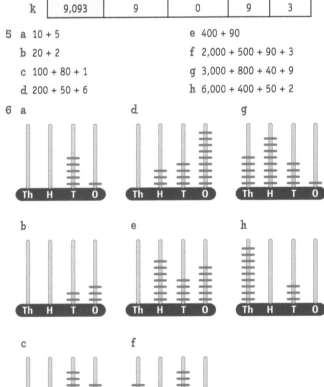

7 a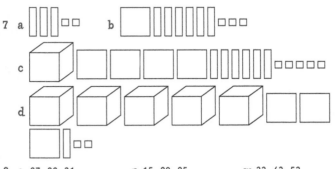

8
a 27, 29, 31	g 15, 20, 25	m 33, 43, 53
b 53, 55, 57	h 55, 50, 45	n 24, 14, 4
c 92, 90, 88	i 70, 60, 50	o 57, 67, 77
d 66, 64, 62	j 50, 60, 70	p 69, 59, 49
e 40, 45, 50	k 20, 10, 0	
f 75, 70, 65	l 100, 110, 120	

9
a + 5	d – 5	g – 3
b + 3	e – 2	h + 4
c + 10	f – 10	

10 a 24; 82; 126; 315; 463
   b 9; 16; 37; 84; 125
   c 65; 91; 124; 347; 1,342
   d 1,011; 1,113; 1,131; 1,311; 3,111

11 a 1,742; 911; 243; 64; 7
   b 1,359; 711; 157; 64; 9
   c 9,501; 3,313; 969; 246; 89
   d 4,232; 3,422; 2,423; 2,243; 2,234

12
	Largest	Smallest
a	543	345
b	874	478
c	954	459
d	921	129
e	733	337
f	944	449

13 a 6,438   c 9,417   e 24   g 6
   b 5,826   d 323   f 246   h 424

14 3 tens (blue cross): 4,235, 37, 333, 630, 8,936
   4 hundreds (green cross): 4,444, 415, 479, 3,421
   2 thousands (purple cross): 2,929, 2,157, 2,349
   8 ones (red cross): 3,348, 28, 8, 58, 258

15 a | 3 | hundreds | 4 | tens | 7 | ones |

   b | 2 | 1 | tens | 5 | ones |

   c | 8 | 7 | 3 | ones |

   d | 3 | hundreds | 7 | tens | 8 | ones |
   | | 3 | 7 | tens | 8 | ones |
   | | | 3 | 7 | 8 | ones |

16 a 3,000   c 3   e 3
   b 30   d 300   f 3

17 a 5   c 5   e 50
   b 5   d 500   f 5,000

18
a False	d True	g True	j False
b True	e False	h True	k True
c True	f True	i True	l False

19 a <   c >   e =   g =   i <
   b >   d <   f >   h >

20 a 10   c 20   e 500   g 630   i 7,490
   b 10   d 120   f 530   h 1,430   j 8,430

21 a 300   c 600   e 6,400
   b 400   d 5,500   f 4,600

22 a 1,000   c 7,000   e 9,000
   b 3,000   d 9,000   f 10,000

23
	Number	Round to nearest 10	Round to nearest 100	Round to nearest 1,000
a	7,493	7,490	7,500	7,000
b	5,812	5,810	5,800	6,000
c	3,567	3,570	3,600	4,000

24 a seventeen
   b twenty-eight
   c one hundred fifty-nine
   d three hundred six
   e five thousand, three hundred forty-two
   f eight thousand, nine hundred nine

2. ADDITION

Adding Numbers to Ten

Page 70 – Example(s)
Example 2: 7, 3, 3

Page 70 – Your Turn
1 a 7   b 6   c 9   d 2
2 a 7 + 3 + 1
   = 10 + 1
   = 11

Page 71 – Practice
1 a 9 + 1 + 2   e 7 + 3 + 5   i 6 + 4 + 5
   = 10 + 2   = 10 + 5   = 10 + 5
   = 12   = 15   = 15

   b 8 + 2 + 5   f 8 + 2 + 8   j 5 + 5 + 6
   = 10 + 5   = 10 + 8   = 10 + 6
   = 15   = 18   = 16

   c 7 + 3 + 7   g 1 + 9 + 8   k 7 + 3 + 6
   = 10 + 7   = 10 + 8   = 10 + 6
   = 17   = 18   = 16

   d 4 + 6 + 9   h 4 + 6 + 7
   = 10 + 9   = 10 + 7
   = 19   = 17

ANSWERS

Adding Numbers to Twenty

Page 72 – Example(s)

$13 + 7 = 20$

Page 72 – Your Turn

$6 + 14 = 20$

Page 73 – Practice

1 a $14 + 6 = 20$

b $3 + 17 = 20$

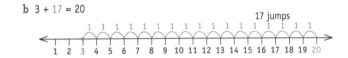

c $2 + 18 = 20$

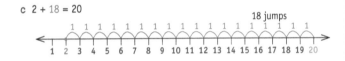

2 a $15 + 5 = 20$

b $19 + 1 = 20$

c $9 + 11 = 20$

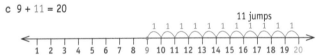

d $8 + 12 = 20$

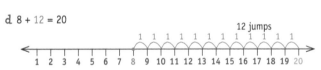

Addition and Subtraction

Page 74 – Example(s)

Example 4: $12 - 3 = 9$

Page 74 – Your Turn

a 4, 11, 7   c 7, 5, 5

b 9, 8, 17   d 13, 7, 13

Page 75 – Practice

1 a 4   b 9   c 0   d 10   e 12

2 a 20, 1, 19   c 16, 14, 16   e 11, 7, 7

b 8, 8, 12   d 5, 5, 8

f $18 - 5 = 13$,
  $5 + 13 = 18$,
  $18 - 13 = 5$

g $16 - 5 = 11$,
  $5 + 11 = 16$,
  $16 - 11 = 5$

h $19 - 2 = 17$,
  $2 + 17 = 19$,
  $19 - 17 = 2$

Jump Strategy to Solve Addition

Page 76 – Example(s)

Example 2

 $63 + 24 = 87$

Page 76 – Your Turn

 $58 + 23 = 81$

Page 77 – Practice

1 a $71 + 15 = 86$

b $27 + 38 = 65$

c $53 + 26 = 79$

d $24 + 35 = 59$

e $33 + 52 = 85$

f $71 + 24 = 95$

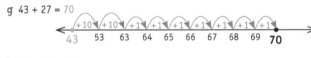

g $43 + 27 = 70$

h $94 + 18 = 112$

Jump Strategy with Larger Numbers

Page 78 – Example(s)

Example 2

$724 + 32 = 756$

Page 78 – Your Turn

$442 + 37 = 479$

Page 79 – Practice

1 a 714 + 25 = 739

   b 327 + 43 = 370

   c 421 + 56 = 477

   d 234 + 73 = 307

   e 843 + 57 = 900

   f 647 + 22 = 669

   g 934 + 31 = 965

   h 133 + 44 = 177

Split Strategy to Solve the Addition of Two-Digit Numbers

Page 80 – Example(s)

Example 2: 30 + 20 ➔ 50 and 2 + 5 = 7

50 + 7

57

Page 80 – Your Turn

63 + 26 ➔ 60 + 20 and 3 + 6 = 9
        = 80 + 9
        = 89

Page 81 – Practice

1 a 28 + 21 ➔ 20 + 20 and 8 + 1
      = 9
      = 40 + 9
      = 49

   b 71 + 14 ➔ 70 + 10 and 1 + 4
      = 5
      = 80 + 5
      = 85

   c 55 + 13 ➔ 50 + 10 and 5 + 3
      = 8
      = 60 + 8
      = 68

   d 51 + 24 ➔ 50 + 20 and 1 + 4
      = 5
      = 70 + 5
      = 75

   e 36 + 12 ➔ 30 + 10 and 6 + 2
      = 8
      = 40 + 8
      = 48

   f 23 + 52 ➔ 20 + 50 and 3 + 2
      = 5
      = 70 + 5
      = 75

Split Strategy to Solve the Addition of Larger Numbers

Page 82 – Example(s)

Example 2: 400 and 30 + 50 = 80 and 5 + 1 = 6

400 + 80 + 6

486

486

Page 82 – Your Turn

   a 724 + 53 ➔ 700 and 20 + 50 = 70 and 4 + 3 = 7
      = 700 + 70 + 7
      = 777

   b 472 + 26 ➔ 400 and 70 + 20 = 90 and 2 + 6 = 8
      = 400 + 90 + 8
      = 498

Page 83 – Practice

1 a 853 + 14 ➔ 800 and 50 + 10 = 60 and 3 + 4 = 7
      = 800 + 60 + 7
      = 867

   b 723 + 56 ➔ 700 and 20 + 50 = 70 and 3 + 6 = 9
      = 700 + 70 + 9
      = 779

   c 642 + 51 ➔ 600 and 40 + 50 = 90 and 2 + 1 = 3
      = 600 + 90 + 3
      = 693

   d 235 + 44 ➔ 200 and 30 + 40 = 70 and 5 + 4 = 9
      = 200 + 70 + 9
      = 279

   e 542 + 27 ➔ 500 and 40 + 20 = 60 and 2 + 7 = 9
      = 500 + 60 + 9
      = 569

   f 143 + 32 ➔ 100 and 40 + 30 = 70 and 3 + 2 = 5
      = 100 + 70 + 5
      = 175

Addition Review Page 84

1 a 3   c 4   e 2
   b 8   d 7   f 5

2 a 3 + 7 + 5 = 15   d 4 + 6 + 1 = 11
   b 9 + 1 + 7 = 17   e 9 + 1 + 0 = 10
   c 8 + 2 + 4 = 14   f 3 + 7 + 8 = 18

3 a 6 + 14 = 20

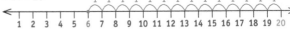

   b 13 + 7 = 20

   c 5 + 17 = 22

   d 16 + 19 = 35

4 a 15, 6, 15, 9   b 20, 12, 12, 20   c 5, 20, 15, 20

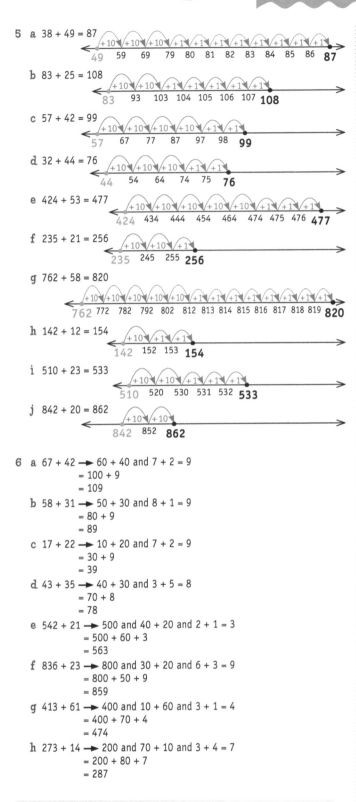

5 a 38 + 49 = 87

b 83 + 25 = 108

c 57 + 42 = 99

d 32 + 44 = 76

e 424 + 53 = 477

f 235 + 21 = 256

g 762 + 58 = 820

h 142 + 12 = 154

i 510 + 23 = 533

j 842 + 20 = 862

6 a 67 + 42 → 60 + 40 and 7 + 2 = 9
    = 100 + 9
    = 109

b 58 + 31 → 50 + 30 and 8 + 1 = 9
    = 80 + 9
    = 89

c 17 + 22 → 10 + 20 and 7 + 2 = 9
    = 30 + 9
    = 39

d 43 + 35 → 40 + 30 and 3 + 5 = 8
    = 70 + 8
    = 78

e 542 + 21 → 500 and 40 + 20 and 2 + 1 = 3
    = 500 + 60 + 3
    = 563

f 836 + 23 → 800 and 30 + 20 and 6 + 3 = 9
    = 800 + 50 + 9
    = 859

g 413 + 61 → 400 and 10 + 60 and 3 + 1 = 4
    = 400 + 70 + 4
    = 474

h 273 + 14 → 200 and 70 + 10 and 3 + 4 = 7
    = 200 + 80 + 7
    = 287

3. SUBTRACTION

Using a Number Line for Subtraction

Page 89 – Example(s)

Example 2

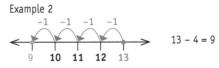

13 – 4 = 9

Page 89 – Your Turn

a 9

b 9

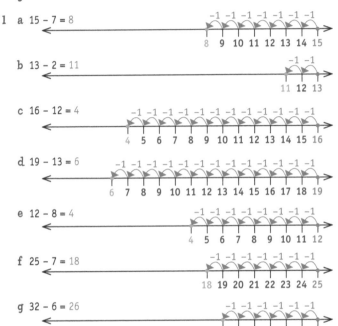

Page 90 – Practice

1 a 15 – 7 = 8

b 13 – 2 = 11

c 16 – 12 = 4

d 19 – 13 = 6

e 12 – 8 = 4

f 25 – 7 = 18

g 32 – 6 = 26

Subtracting Numbers from Ten

Page 91 – Example(s)

Example 2: 10 – 7 = 3; 7, 3

Page 91 – Your Turn

a 8   c 6   e 4

b 9   d 1   f 10

Page 92 – Practice

1 a 10 – 6 = 4

b 10 – 9 = 1

c 10 – 0 = 10

d 10 – 5 = 5

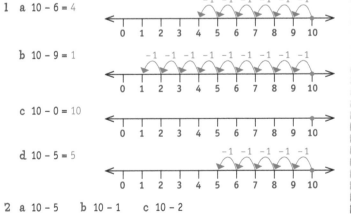

2 a 10 – 5   b 10 – 1   c 10 – 2

Subtracting Numbers from Twenty Using a Number Line

Page 93 – Example(s)

Example 2: 7

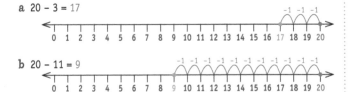

Page 93 – Your Turn

a 20 – 3 = 17

b 20 – 11 = 9

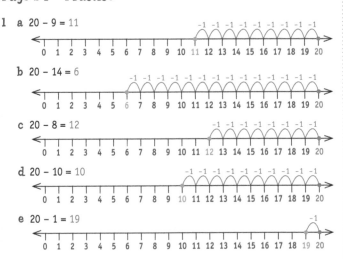

Page 94 – Practice

1 a 20 – 9 = 11

b 20 – 14 = 6

c 20 – 8 = 12

d 20 – 10 = 10

e 20 – 1 = 19

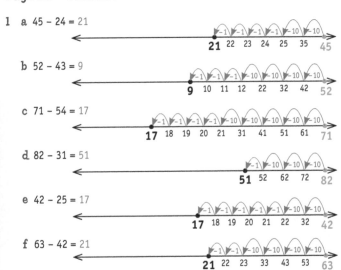

Jump Strategy with Two-Digit Numbers

Page 95 – Example(s)

Example 2
68 – 42 = 26

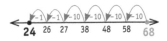

Page 95 – Your Turn

73 – 15 = 58

Page 96 – Practice

1 a 45 – 24 = 21

b 52 – 43 = 9

c 71 – 54 = 17

d 82 – 31 = 51

e 42 – 25 = 17

f 63 – 42 = 21

Jump Strategy with Larger Numbers

Page 97 — Example(s)

Example 2
724 – 32 = 692

Page 97 – Your Turn

a 523 – 41 = 482

b 714 – 29 = 685

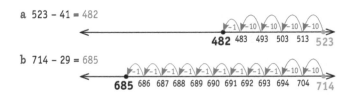

Page 98 – Practice

1 a 524 – 33 = 491

b 647 – 28 = 619

c 421 – 56 = 365

d 284 – 41 = 243

e 934 – 42 = 892

f 873 – 67 = 806

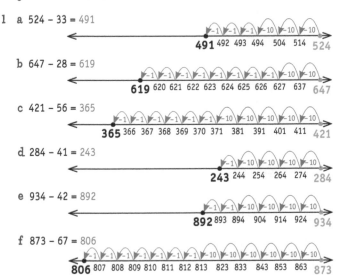

Subtraction Using the Split Strategy

Page 99 – Example(s)

Example 2: 70 – 20 → 50 and 4 – 3 = 1
50 + 1
51

Page 99 – Your Turn

74 – 33 → 70 – 30 = 40 and 4 – 3 = 1
= 40 + 1
= 41

Page 100 – Practice

1 a 72 – 31 → 70 – 30 = 40 and
2 – 1 = 1
= 40 + 1
= 41

b 58 – 24 → 50 – 20 = 30 and
8 – 4 = 4
= 30 + 4
= 34

c 64 – 41 → 60 – 40 = 20 and
4 – 1 = 3
= 20 + 3
= 23

d 93 – 52 → 90 – 50 = 40 and
3 – 2 = 1
= 40 + 1
= 41

e 43 – 22 → 40 – 20 = 20 and 3 – 2 = 1
= 20 + 1
= 21

f 68 – 27 → 60 – 20 = 40 and 8 – 7 = 1
= 40 + 1
= 41

Subtraction Using the Split Strategy with Larger Numbers

Page 101 – Example(s)

Example 2: 30 – 20 → 10 and 5 – 3 = 2
700 + 10 + 2
712

Page 101 – Your Turn

a 684 – 53 ➤ 600 and 80 – 50 = 30 and 4 – 3 = 1
    = 600 + 30 + 1
    = 631

Page 102 – Practice

1 a 859 – 38 ➤ 800 and 50 – 30 = 20 and 9 – 8 = 1
        = 800 + 20 + 1
        = 821

   b 586 – 43 ➤ 500 and 80 – 40 = 40 and 6 – 3 = 3
        = 500 + 40 + 3
        = 543

   c 747 – 35 ➤ 700 and 40 – 30 = 10 and 7 – 5 = 2
        = 700 + 10 + 2
        = 712

   d 572 – 51 ➤ 500 and 70 – 50 = 20 and 2 – 1 = 1
        = 500 + 20 + 1
        = 521

   e 732 – 11 ➤ 700 and 30 – 10 = 20 and 2 – 1 = 1
        = 700 + 20 + 1
        = 721

   f 457 – 26 ➤ 400 and 50 – 20 = 30 and 7 – 6 = 1
        = 400 + 30 + 1
        = 431

Subtraction Review Page 103

1 a 15 – 8 = 7

   b 14 – 3 = 11

   c 27 – 5 = 22

   d 39 – 3 = 36

2 a 7   c 10   e 18
   b 4   d 7   f 13

3 a 68 – 47 = 21

   b 84 – 21 = 63

   c 76 – 32 = 44

   d 856 – 24 = 832

   e 925 – 13 = 912

   f 737 – 25 = 712

4 a 58 – 35 ➤ 50 – 30 = 20 and 8 – 5 = 3
        = 20 + 3
        = 23

   b 67 – 42 ➤ 60 – 40 = 20 and 7 – 2 = 5
        = 20 + 5
        = 25

   c 83 – 22 ➤ 80 – 20 = 60 and 3 – 2 = 1
        = 60 + 1
        = 61

   d 57 – 36 ➤ 50 – 30 = 20 and 7 – 6 = 1
        = 20 + 1
        = 21

   e 937 – 25 ➤ 900 and 30 – 20 = 10 and 7 – 5 = 2
        = 900 + 10 + 2
        = 912

   f 638 – 27 ➤ 600 and 30 – 20 = 10 and 8 – 7 = 1
        = 600 + 10 + 1
        = 611

   g 762 – 41 ➤ 700 and 60 – 40 = 20 and 2 – 1 = 1
        = 700 + 20 + 1
        = 721

   h 478 – 65 ➤ 400 and 70 – 60 = 10 and 8 – 5 = 3
        = 400 + 10 + 3
        = 413

4. MULTIPLICATION

Groups and Rows

Page 106 – Example(s)

Example 3: 2 groups of 7

Page 106 – Your Turn

1 a 3 rows of 2
2 a 4 groups of 3

Page 107 – Practice

1 a 3   b 1

2 a 3   b 4

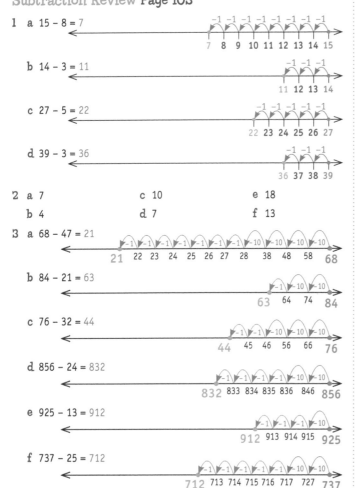

3 a   c

   b

4 a   c

   b

Repeated Addition

Page 108 – Example(s)

Example 2: 3 rows of 2 = 6
2 + 2 + 2 = 6
3 × 2 = 6

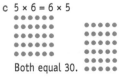

Page 108 – Your Turn

a 2 groups of 5 = 10
5 + 5 = 10
2 × 5 = 10

b 2 groups of 4 = 8
4 + 4 = 8
2 × 4 = 8

c 4 rows of 3 = 12
3 + 3 + 3 + 3 = 12
4 × 3 = 12

Page 109 – Practice

1 a

b (•) (•) (•)

c (••)(••) (••)(••) (••)(••) (••)(••)

2 a (•••••) (•••••) (•••••)

3 groups of 5 = 15
5 + 5 + 5 = 15
3 × 5 = 15

b (••) (••) (••) (••) (••)

5 groups of 2 = 10
2 + 2 + 2 + 2 + 2 = 10
5 × 2 = 10

c
•••
•••
•••
•••

4 rows of 3 = 12
3 + 3 + 3 + 3 = 12
4 × 3 = 12

d
•
•
•
•
•

5 rows of 1 = 5
1 + 1 + 1 + 1 + 1 = 5
5 × 1 = 5

e (•••••) (•••••)

2 groups of 10 = 20
10 + 10 = 20
2 × 10 = 20

Commutative Property

Page 110 – Example(s)

Example 2: 4 × 5 = 5 × 4
Both equal 20.

Page 110 – Your Turn

a

Both equal 12.

Page 111 – Practice

1 a 2 × 5 = 5 × 2

Both equal 10.

b 3 × 6 = 6 × 3

Both equal 18.

c 5 × 6 = 6 × 5

Both equal 30.

2 a 2 × 6 = 6 × 2
b 4 × 3 = 3 × 4
c 5 × 2 = 2 × 5
d 10 × 3 = 3 × 10
e 5 × 7 = 7 × 5
f 6 × 1 = 1 × 6
g 2 × 7 = 7 × 2

The Inverse Operations of Multiplication and Division

Page 112 – Example(s)

Example 2:

Words		Number sentence
2 rows of 7 equals 14	➡	2 × 7 = 14
7 groups of 2 equals 14	➡	7 × 2 = 14
14 shared into 2 rows equals 7	➡	14 ÷ 2 = 7
14 shared into 2 groups equals 7	➡	14 ÷ 7 = 2

Page 112 – Your Turn

3 rows of 2 equals 6	➡	3 × 2 = 6
2 groups of 3 equals 6	➡	2 × 3 = 6
6 shared into 2 rows equals 3	➡	6 ÷ 2 = 3
6 shared into 3 groups equals 2	➡	6 ÷ 3 = 2

Page 113 – Practice

1 a 5 × 3 = 15
b 3 × 5 = 15
c 15 ÷ 3 = 5
d 15 ÷ 5 = 3

2 a 18 ÷ 3 = 6 or 18 ÷ 6 = 3
b 10 × 2 = 20 or 2 × 10 = 20
c 18 ÷ 9 = 2 or 18 ÷ 2 = 9
d 2 × 12 = 24 or 12 × 2 = 24
e 1 × 12 = 12 or 12 × 1 = 12
f 21 ÷ 3 = 7 or 21 ÷ 7 = 3
g 35 ÷ 5 = 7 or 35 ÷ 7 = 5

3 a 15 ÷ 3 = 5
b 24 ÷ 8 = 3
c 20 ÷ 4 = 5
d 22 ÷ 11 = 2
e 36 ÷ 12 = 3

Multiplication Review Page 114

1 a 2   b 3   c 5

2 a 2   b 1   c 3

3 a 4 groups of 3
3 + 3 + 3 + 3 = 12
4 × 3 = 12

b 3 groups of 5
5 + 5 + 5 = 15
3 × 5 = 15

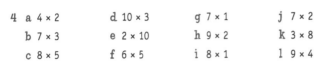

4 a 4 × 2   d 10 × 3   g 7 × 1   j 7 × 2
   b 7 × 3   e 2 × 10   h 9 × 2   k 3 × 8
   c 8 × 5   f 6 × 5   i 8 × 1   l 9 × 4

5 a

Words	Number sentence
4 rows of 5 equals 20	4 × 5 = 20
5 groups of 4 equals 20	5 × 4 = 20
20 shared into 4 rows equals 5	20 ÷ 4 = 5
20 shared into 5 groups equals 4	20 ÷ 5 = 4

   b

Words	Number sentence
3 rows of 8 equals 24	3 × 8 = 24
8 groups of 3 equals 24	8 × 3 = 24
24 shared into 3 rows equals 8	24 ÷ 3 = 8
24 shared into 8 groups equals 3	24 ÷ 8 = 3

6 a 21 ÷ 7 = 3 or 21 ÷ 3 = 7   d 18 ÷ 3 = 6 or 18 ÷ 6 = 3
   b 12 ÷ 6 = 2 or 12 ÷ 2 = 6   e 12 ÷ 1 = 12 or 12 ÷ 12 = 1
   c 20 ÷ 4 = 5 or 20 ÷ 5 = 4   f 35 ÷ 5 = 7 or 35 ÷ 7 = 5
7 a 8 ÷ 2 = 4   c 60 ÷ 5 = 12
   b 22 ÷ 2 = 11   d 40 ÷ 4 = 10

5. DIVISION

Groups

Page 116 – Example(s)
Example 3: 6 groups of 3 stars

Page 116 – Your Turn
   a 3 groups of 3   b 5 groups of 3

Page 117 – Practice
1 a 4 groups of 2, 3 groups of 2, 1 group of 2
   b 4 groups of 3, 1 group of 3, 6 groups of 3
   c 4 groups of 5, 2 groups of 5, 1 group of 5
   d 3 groups of 10, 2 groups of 10, 4 groups of 10

Division by Equal Shares

Page 118 – Example(s)
Example 2: These 8 cupcakes are shared equally between 2 people.
Each person gets 4 cupcakes.

Page 118 – Your Turn
   a 5

Page 119 – Practice
1 a 4 flowers in each box   c 5 crayons in each box
   b 3 starfish in each box   d 3 orange slices on each plate
2 The wrong words are:
   a unequal   c equal   e unequal
   b unequal   d equal

Division by Grouping

Page 120 – Example(s)
Example 3: 6, 3

Page 120 – Your Turn
   a 5, 4

Page 121 – Practice
1 a 2, 3   b 4, 3   c 6, 5

2 a

   b

   c

Division

Page 122 – Example(s)
Example 2: 5, 4, 5
20 ÷ 4 = 5

Page 122 – Your Turn
   a 4, 12 ÷ 3 = 4

Page 123 – Practice
1 a 5, 5   b 4, 4   c 5, 5

2 a 5, 5   b 7, 7   c 4, 4

Remainders

Page 124 – Example(s)
Example 2: 4, 2

Page 124 – Your Turn
   a Each person gets 8 pencils and there is 1 remainder.
      17 ÷ 2 = 8 remainder 1

Page 125 – Practice
1 a 9, 1 remainder, 19 ÷ 2 = 9 remainder 1
   b 4, 1 remainder, 21 ÷ 5 = 4 remainder 1
   c 3, 2 remainder, 14 ÷ 4 = 3 remainder 2
   d 11, 1 remainder, 23 ÷ 2 = 11 remainder 1

Repeated Subtraction to Solve Division

Page 126 – Example(s)
Example 2:
21
18
15
12
9
6
3
24 ÷ 3 = 8
8 times, so the answer is 8

Page 126 – Your Turn
   a 15 ÷ 3 = 5
      15 − 3 = 12
      12 − 3 = 9
      9 − 3 = 6
      6 − 3 = 3
      3 − 3 = 0
      5 times

Page 127 – Practice

1 a 12 ÷ 2 = 6
      12 − 2 = 10
      10 − 2 = 8
      8 − 2 = 6
      6 − 2 = 4
      4 − 2 = 2
      2 − 2 = 0
      6 times

   b 20 ÷ 5 = 4
      20 − 5 = 15
      15 − 5 = 10
      10 − 5 = 5
      5 − 5 = 0
      4 times

   c 30 ÷ 10 = 3
      30 − 10 = 20
      20 − 10 = 10
      10 − 10 = 0
      3 times

   d 21 ÷ 3 = 7
      21 − 3 = 18
      18 − 3 = 15
      15 − 3 = 12
      12 − 3 = 9
      9 − 3 = 6
      6 − 3 = 3
      3 − 3 = 0
      7 times

   e 30 ÷ 5 = 6
      30 − 5 = 25
      25 − 5 = 20
      20 − 5 = 15
      15 − 5 = 10
      10 − 5 = 5
      5 − 5 = 0
      6 times

Division Review Page 128

1 a 3, 2   b 5, 2   c 10, 2

2 a 3 fish in each group   c 5 balls in each group
   b 4 kiwi slices in each group

3 Wrong word:
   a unequal   b equal   c equal

4 a 3, 4   b 5, 5   c 6, 2   d 8, 3

5 a 12 ÷ 2 = 6   b 20 ÷ 4 = 5   c 18 ÷ 6 = 3   d 24 ÷ 3 = 8

6 a 20 shared among 10 = 2   c 35 shared among 7 = 5
      20 ÷ 10 = 2   35 ÷ 7 = 5
   b 15 shared among 5 = 3
      15 ÷ 5 = 3

7 a 5, 2   b 6, 0

8 a 24 ÷ 4 = 6
      24 − 4 = 20
      20 − 4 = 16
      16 − 4 = 12
      12 − 4 = 8
      8 − 4 = 4
      4 − 4 = 0
      6 times

   b 12 ÷ 2 = 6
      12 − 2 = 10
      10 − 2 = 8
      8 − 2 = 6
      6 − 2 = 4
      4 − 2 = 2
      2 − 2 = 0
      6 times

   c 15 ÷ 5 = 3
      15 − 5 = 10
      10 − 5 = 5
      5 − 5 = 0
      3 times

   d 35 ÷ 5 = 7
      35 − 5 = 30
      30 − 5 = 25
      25 − 5 = 20
      20 − 5 = 15
      15 − 5 = 10
      10 − 5 = 5
      5 − 5 = 0
      7 times

   e 40 ÷ 8 = 5
      40 − 8 = 32
      32 − 8 = 24
      24 − 8 = 16
      16 − 8 = 8
      8 − 8 = 0
      5 times

6. FRACTIONS

Fractions—Halves

Page 132 – Example(s)

Example 2

Page 132 – Your Turn

Circled:

c   d   e   g   h

Page 133 – Practice

1 b, c, d, e, h
2 (possible answers)

a   b   c

d   e   f

3 a   b   c

Fractions—Quarters and Eighths

Page 134 – Example(s)

Example 2   Example 3

Page 134 – Your Turn

Quarters: c, d   Eighths: b, f, h

Page 135 – Practice

1 Possible answers:

Quarters

Eighths

2

	Fraction name	Fraction	Color the Fraction
a	one-quarter	$\frac{1}{4}$	
b	three-eighths	$\frac{3}{8}$	
c	three-quarters	$\frac{3}{4}$	
d	five-eighths	$\frac{5}{8}$	
e	two-quarters	$\frac{2}{4}$	

3 Possible answers:

a   b   c   d

Fractions—Thirds and Fifths

Page 136 – Example(s)

Example 3   Example 4

ANSWERS

Page 136 – Your Turn

Page 137 – Practice

1 Thirds:

2 Fifths:

3

	Fraction name	Fraction	Picture
a	two-thirds	$\frac{2}{3}$	
b	one-third	$\frac{1}{3}$	
c	four-fifths	$\frac{4}{5}$	

Half of a Collection
Page 138 – Example(s)
Example 2: 5, 5
Page 138 – Your Turn
3 balls each
Page 139 – Practice

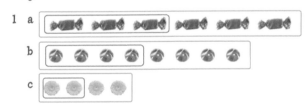

2 a 3, 6 b 10, 20 c 12, 24 d 5, 10 e 4, 8

Quarters and Eighths of a Collection
Page 140 – Example(s)
Example 3: 3, 3
Page 140 – Your Turn
2, 2
Page 141 – Practice

3 a eighths, 3, 24   c eighths, 1, 8

$\frac{1}{8}$ of 24 = 3 $\frac{1}{8}$ of 8 = 1

b quarters, 2, 8

$\frac{1}{4}$ of 8 = 2

Thirds and Fifths of a Collection
Page 142 – Example(s)
Example 3: 3
Page 142 – Your Turn
a 6, 6   b 5, 5
Page 143 – Practice

1 a 2   b 5   c 1

2 a 2   b 4   c 1

3 a 4, 12, 12, 4   c 6, 30, 30, 6
 b 2, 10, 10, 2

Comparing Fractions
Page 144 – Example(s)
Example 3: Possible answer: $\frac{1}{4}$

Example 4: Possible answer: $\frac{1}{8}$

Page 144 – Your Turn
a False   b False   c False

Page 145 – Practice

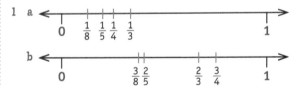

2 a $\frac{2}{8}$, $\frac{6}{8}$
 b $\frac{7}{8}$, $\frac{1}{8}$

3 a $\frac{8}{10}$, $\frac{6}{10}$, $\frac{5}{10}$, $\frac{3}{10}$, $\frac{1}{10}$ c $\frac{1}{2}$, $\frac{1}{3}$, $\frac{1}{4}$, $\frac{1}{5}$, $\frac{1}{8}$
 b $\frac{34}{100}$, $\frac{24}{100}$, $\frac{17}{100}$, $\frac{13}{100}$, $\frac{5}{100}$

4 $\frac{1}{4}$ $\frac{1}{3}$ $\frac{1}{2}$ $\frac{1}{5}$ $\frac{1}{8}$

3 4 5 2 1

5 a <   c >   e >   g >
 b <   d <   f <   h >

6 a 6   b 8   c 12   d $\frac{1}{2}$ e $\frac{1}{4}$

7 a $\frac{1}{2}$ c $\frac{9}{10}$ e $\frac{4}{5}$ g $\frac{3}{4}$
 b $\frac{7}{8}$ d $\frac{9}{10}$ f $\frac{2}{3}$ h $\frac{7}{8}$

ANSWERS

8 a $\frac{3}{8}$ c $\frac{3}{10}$ e $\frac{3}{8}$ g $\frac{2}{4}$

   b $\frac{1}{3}$ d $\frac{2}{5}$ f $\frac{2}{5}$ h $\frac{3}{8}$

Fractions Review **Page 147**

1 halves

   quarters

   eighths   thirds

   fifths

2 a   b   c   d   e

   $\frac{2}{3}$ $\frac{3}{5}$ $\frac{3}{4}$ $\frac{1}{2}$ $\frac{7}{8}$

3 a two-fifths $\frac{2}{5}$ c one-third $\frac{1}{3}$

   b five-eighths $\frac{5}{8}$ d one-quarter $\frac{1}{4}$

4 a $\frac{1}{2}$ of 12 = 6   d $\frac{1}{2}$ of 10 = 5

   b $\frac{1}{2}$ of 8 = 4   e $\frac{1}{2}$ of 12 = 6

   c $\frac{1}{2}$ of 4 = 2   f $\frac{1}{2}$ of 20 = 10

5 a 5, 10   b 1, 2   c 12, 24   d 3, 6

6 a 8, 2   b 12, 3   c 4, 1   d 20, 5

7 a 2   b 1   c 4

8 b, d

9 15, 5

10 20, 4

11 a $\frac{2}{5}, \frac{3}{4}, \frac{7}{8}$, 1 whole   b $\frac{3}{8}, \frac{2}{3}, \frac{6}{8}, \frac{4}{5}$

12 a

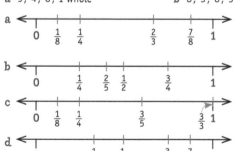

13 a >   c <   e >   g <   i >
   b <   d <   f >   h <

14 3, 4, 6

15 a $\frac{2}{3}, \boxed{\frac{3}{5}}, \frac{4}{8}$ e $\frac{1}{5}, \frac{5}{8}, \boxed{\frac{3}{4}}$

   b $\frac{1}{2}, \boxed{\frac{3}{4}}, \frac{2}{5}$ f $\frac{3}{5}, \boxed{\frac{7}{8}}, \frac{3}{4}$

   c $\boxed{\frac{2}{3}}, \frac{1}{4}, \frac{3}{5}$ g $\frac{2}{3}, \frac{3}{4}, \boxed{\frac{7}{8}}$

   d $\frac{4}{5}, \frac{1}{2}, \boxed{\frac{7}{8}}$ h $\frac{1}{4}, \frac{1}{2}, \boxed{1\ whole}$

7. DATA

Data and Tables

Page 152 – Example(s)

Example 2

Room 4's Favorite Sports

Bird	Tally	Total
Blue Jay	卌 I	6
Crow	卌 卌 I	11
Cardinal	卌 I	6
Dove	卌	5
Sparrow	卌 卌	10
Seagull	卌 卌 IIII	14
		52

Page 152 – Your Turn

a Tacos   c Pasta, Pizza

b Fish and chips   d 22

Page 153 – Practice

1 a   Room 4's Favorite Sports

Sport	Tally	Total
Soccer	卌 II	7
Football	卌 III	8
Tennis	卌	5
Basketball	III	3
		23

   b   Room 4's Favorite Ice Cream

Ice Cream	Tally	Total
Chocolate	卌 III	8
Vanilla	卌 卌	10
Strawberry	I	1
Caramel	IIII	4
Mint	II	2
		25

c
Room 4's Favorite Fruits

Fruit	Tally	Total
Apple	|||	3
Mango	⊬⊬⊬ ⊬⊬⊬ ||||	14
Banana	⊬⊬⊬ |||	8
Watermelon	⊬⊬⊬		6
Grapes	||	2
		33

2 a Sunday   e 5
   b Monday   f 0
   c Wednesday and Thursday   g 7
   d 10

Picture Graphs

Page 155 – Example(s)

a 2

b April, October, and November

c May or September; July; August

Page 156 – Your Turn

1 a 7   c 6   e Motorcycles
   b 4   d Cars

2
Room 5's Favorite Ways to Travel

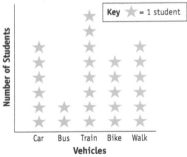

Page 157 – Practice

1
Lucas's Activities in May

Activity	Tally	Total
Surfing	||	2
Swim	⊬⊬⊬	5
Band	⊬⊬⊬	5
Art	⊬⊬⊬	5
Soccer	⊬⊬⊬ |||	8
Drama	|||	3
		28

2
Lucas's Activities in May

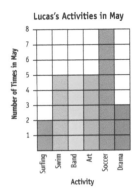

3 a Soccer   c 3
   b Surfing   d 5

4 a 1   c 3   e 5   g 24
   b 4   d dogs   f 12   h 4

5
Number of Books Read in Semester 1

Name	Tally	Total
Dylan	⊬⊬⊬ ⊬⊬⊬ ⊬⊬⊬	15
Jacob	⊬⊬⊬ ⊬⊬⊬	10
Annie	⊬⊬⊬ ⊬⊬⊬ ⊬⊬⊬ ⊬⊬⊬ ⊬⊬⊬ ⊬⊬⊬	30
Christian	⊬⊬⊬ ⊬⊬⊬ ⊬⊬⊬ ⊬⊬⊬ ⊬⊬⊬	25
Antonia	⊬⊬⊬ ⊬⊬⊬ ⊬⊬⊬ ⊬⊬⊬ ⊬⊬⊬ ⊬⊬⊬	30
Allan	⊬⊬⊬ ⊬⊬⊬ ⊬⊬⊬ ⊬⊬⊬	20
Danny	⊬⊬⊬	5
		135

a 20   c 25
b Danny   d Annie and Antonia

6
Rolls

Number	Tally	Total
⚀	⊬⊬⊬	5
⚁	||||	4
⚂	⊬⊬⊬	5
⚃	||	2
⚄	⊬⊬⊬		6
⚅	||||	4
		26

a 5
b 4
c 4
d 1
e 26

7 a
Cars That Passed Our School

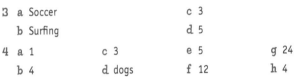

b Answers should reflect three things students learned from the survey.
Sample answer: I learned that a key explains what the pictures mean in
a picture graph.

Bar Graphs

Page 162 – Example(s)

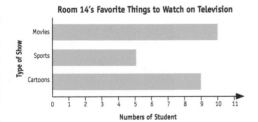

Room 14's Favorite Things to Watch on Television

Page 163 – Your Turn

a Walk
b Car
c 1
d 5
e Motorcycle and Taxi
f 5
g 29

Page 164 – Practice

1 a Banana
   b 10
   c Mango
   d 9
   e 3

2

Room 9's Favorite Fruits

Type of Fruit	Tally	Total
Apple	|||||	5
Orange	||||| |||	8
Strawberry	||||| |||||	10
Banana	||	2
Mango	||||| |||||		11
		36

3

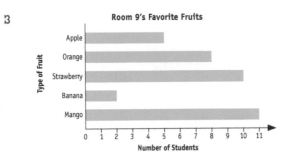

Room 9's Favorite Fruits

4 Answers should reflect three questions students could ask their friends using the information from the graph.

5 a Action
   b Horror
   c Drama, Thriller
   d less
   e less
   f 8

Data Review Page 167

1

Room 12's Favorite Colors

Color	Tally	Total
Black	||	2
Red	|||||	5
Orange	|||	3
Blue	||||| |||||	10
		20

a 2
b Blue
c Black
d 5

2

Room 15's Favorite Fruits

Type of Fruit	Tally	Total
Banana	||	2
Mango	|||||	5
Cherries	||||| |||||	10
Watermelon	||||| ||||| ||	12
		29

3

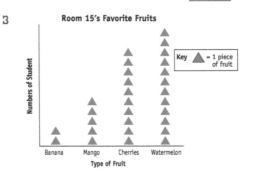

Room 15's Favorite Fruits

Key △ = 1 piece of fruit

4

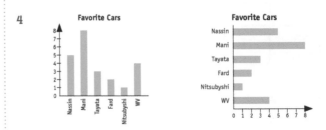

Favorite Cars   **Favorite Cars**

8. LENGTH

Informal Units

Page 170 – Example(s)

b 4
c 8

Page 170 – Your Turn

1 a 5
   b 4
   c shorter
   d shortest

Page 171 – Practice

1 red: 6   orange: 2   green: 4   blue: 8

2 a shorter   b longer   c shorter

3 a red   c 7   e 6
   b 8   d green

4 2 green, 1 yellow, 3 orange

5 a 3 bricks   b 5 bricks   c 1 brick   d 2 bricks

6 a orange   c 1 or 2   e longer
   b yellow   d longer

Meters and Feet

Page 174 – Example(s)

Mark horse, bus, car, and bicycle.

Page 174 – Your Turn

1 a–e

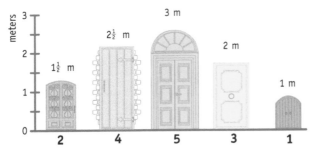

f 2 m

Page 175 – Practice

1 House A: 2 ft., House B: 2½ ft., House C: 1½ ft.,
House D: 3 ft., House E: 2 ft.

2 a House C   c 2½ ft.   e 1 ft.

b 2 ft.   d 1½ ft.   f E

3 a

Name	Measurement (m)	Measurement (cm)	Place
Ally	1½ m	150 cm	2nd
Hazel	1 m	100 cm	3rd
Amber	2 m	200 cm	1st

b Amber   c Hazel

4 Adult to check

5 Adult to check

Centimeters and Inches

Page 177 – Example(s)

b 6 in.   d 2 in.

c 10 cm   e 8 cm

Page 177 – Your Turn

a 2, 5, 4, 1, 3   c 2 cm

b 4 in.   d longer

Page 178 – Practice

1 a 7 cm   b 4 cm   c 11 cm   d 5 cm   e 6 cm

2 a 3 in.   b 2 in.   c 1½ in.   d 2½ in.   e 4½ in.

Length Review Page 179

1 Blue: 1 Green: 4 Red: 3 Pink: 2

2 a shortest   b shorter   c longest

3 3, 4, 1, 2, 5

4 a 5 cm   b 8 cm   c 11 cm   d 3 cm

5 a feet   b inches   c feet   d inches   e inches

6 a 3 in.   b 4 in.   c 2 in.   d 5 in.

9. SHAPES

Triangles

Page 181 – Example(s)

a red   c blue

b green   d green

Page 181 – Your Turn

Color c, d, g

Page 182 – Practice

1 Adult to check

2 Adult to check

3 a check mark (regular)   e X (irregular)

b X (irregular)   f X (irregular)

c X (irregular)   g check mark (regular)

d check mark (regular)   h X (irregular)

Quadrilaterals

Page 183 – Example(s)

a orange   c green   e yellow

b blue   d red

Page 183 – Your Turn

Page 184 – Practice

1 a   e

b   f

c   g

d

2 Adult to check

3

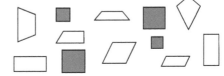

Pentagons and Hexagons

Page 185 – Example(s)
b irregular hexagon   d regular hexagon

c irregular hexagon

Page 185 – Your Turn

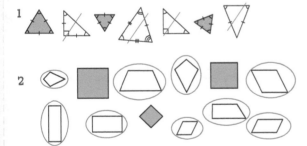

Page 186 – Practice

1

2 Adult to check

3

Shape	Regular pentagon	Irregular pentagon	Regular hexagon	Irregular hexagon
Diagram				
Number of corners	5	5	6	6
Number of sides	5	5	6	6

Shapes Review Page 187

1

2

3

Shape	Diagram	No. corners	No. sides
regular pentagon		5	5
irregular pentagon	various	5	5
regular hexagon		6	6
irregular hexagon	various	6	6

10. AREA

Measuring Area with Units

Page 188 – Example(s)
b 35

Page 188 – Your Turn

a 20   b 12

Page 189 – Practice

1   a no spaces   c spaces   e no spaces

   b no spaces   d no spaces

2   a 28   c 4

   b *Garden Girl, Bobby B. Brown*

Measuring Area with a Grid

Page 190 – Example(s)
b 12, 14

Page 190 – Your Turn

a 35

Page 191 – Practice

1   a 15   b 25   c 21, 6, 24

2   *Mountain Bikes*: 15 squares   a *Cheer*

   Cheer: 30 squares   b *Top Travel Spots*

   Top Travel Spots: 6 squares   c 18 squares

   Pets Are Perfect: 12 squares   d 9 squares

Square Centimeters and Square Inches

Page 192 – Example(s)
b 9, 9

Page 192 – Your Turn

a 8, 8   b 5, 5

Page 193 – Practice

1

Shape	Area in words	Area using cm²
A	four square centimeters	4 cm²
B	eleven square centimeters	11 cm²
C	six square centimeters	6 cm²
D	four square centimeters	4 cm²
E	ten square centimeters	10 cm²
F	one square centimeter	1 cm²

2   a 1 cm²   c C   e E

   b A, D   d 10 cm²

Square Meters and Square Feet

Page 194 – Example(s)
b 5   c 6

Page 194 – Your Turn
Circle pencil case and book

Page 195 – Practice

1 a 12   b 6   c 9   d 8

2 Circle garage door, elevator doors, sofa

3 Adult to check

Area Review Page 196

1 a 12   b 20   c 20   d 25

2 Mark a, b, e, g

3 a 24   b 6   c 18, 6, 21

4 a 10, 10   b 21, 21   c 14, 14   d 9, 9

5 Circle phone, sticky note, and dollar
   Cross out bookcase, desk, and window

6 Circle book and plate.
   Cross out basketball court, door, bowling alley, road.

7 a 16 m²   c 53 m²   e 49 m²   g 826 m²
   b 103 m²   d 84 m²   f 109 m²   h 87 m²

11. CAPACITY

Capacity

Page 199 – Example(s)

b Answers should have smaller capacity than given container.

c Answers should have smaller capacity than given container.

Page 199 – Your Turn

a Circle middle object, cross out right object
b Circle middle object, cross out left object
c Circle middle object, cross out right object

Page 200 – Practice

1 a Circle right object   b Circle right object   c Circle left object

2 a pitcher   b 4   c 2   d smaller

Comparing Capacity

Page 201 – Example(s)

b 2, 4, 1, 3, 5

Page 201 – Your Turn

1 a Circle middle container   b Circle right container
   c Circle left container

Page 202 – Practice

1 a Cross out middle object   b Cross out right object
   c Cross out right object

2 a Circle right object   d Circle right object   g Circle right object
   b Circle left object   e Circle left object
   c Circle right object   f Circle right object

Liters and Gallons

Page 203 – Example(s)

b 5 gallons   d 4 liters
c 1 gallon   e 2 liters

Page 203 – Your Turn

a 12 gal.   c 3 gal.   e 4 L
b 1 L   d 7 gal.

Page 204 – Practice

1 a more than   c less than   e less than
   b more than   d less than

2 Cross out a, c, e

3 Check pool, wheelbarrow, cooler

Measuring Liquids

Page 205 – Example(s)

Page 205 – Your Turn

a 2 L   b 3 L

Page 206 – Practice

1 a three liters 3 L   b four liters 4 L   c two liters 2 L

2 a   b   c

3 a

   b

Capacity Review Page 207

1 a Circle left container   c Circle left container
   b Circle left container   d Circle right container

2 a 1, 4, 5, 2, 3   b 3, 4, 1, 5, 2   c 4, 3, 5, 2, 1

3 a Circle left container, cross out right container
   b Circle right container, cross out middle container
   c Circle left container, cross out right container
   d Circle right container, cross out left container

4 a 4 L   c 12 L   e 7 L
   b 6 gal.   d 15 gal.   f 19 gal.

5 a less   b more   c less

6 Adult to check

7 a 2 L   c 1 L   e 4 L
   b 2 L   d 5 L   f 9 L

8 a   b   c

d   e   f

12. MASS

Page 210 – Example(s)

b lighter than   c lighter than

Page 210 – Your Turn

a dog on right   b cookies on left   c blocks on right

Page 211 – Practice

1 a black box   c pink box   e green box
  b green box   d orange box

2 Mark c, d, e

3 a Ravi is lighter than Joe.   c Kim is lighter than Nia.
  b Kala is the same mass as Ray.   d Zeb is heavier than Kai.

Kilograms and Pounds

Page 212 – Example(s)

Page 212 – Your Turn

Mark b, c, g

Page 213 – Practice

1 a | 10 lbs. | 10 lbs. | 10 lbs. | 5 lbs. | 5 lbs. | 5 lbs. | 1 lb. | 1 lb. | 1 lb. |
| 10 lbs. | 10 lbs. | 10 lbs. | 5 lbs. | 5 lbs. | 5 lbs. | 1 lb. | 1 lb. | 1 lb. |

b | 10 kg | 10 kg | 10 kg | 5 kg | 5 kg | 5 kg | 1 kg | 1 kg | 1 kg |
| 10 kg | 10 kg | 10 kg | 5 kg | 5 kg | 5 kg | 1 kg | 1 kg | 1 kg |

c | 10 lbs. | 10 lbs. | 10 lbs. | 5 lbs. | 5 lbs. | 5 lbs. | 1 lb. | 1 lb. | 1 lb. |
| 10 lbs. | 10 lbs. | 10 lbs. | 5 lbs. | 5 lbs. | 5 lbs. | 1 lb. | 1 lb. | 1 lb. |

d | 10 kg | 10 kg | 10 kg | 5 kg | 5 kg | 5 kg | 1 kg | 1 kg | 1 kg |
| 10 kg | 10 kg | 10 kg | 5 kg | 5 kg | 5 kg | 1 kg | 1 kg | 1 kg |

2 a 34   b 58   c 27   d 79

3 a 7 kg   c 24 kg   e 28 kg
  b 9 lbs.   d 32 lbs.   f 43 lbs.

4 a 1 kg   c 10 kg   e oranges,   f 2 kg
  b 4 kg   d bananas   apples, grapes   g pineapple

5 a 12 lbs.   c rice and steak   e 3 bags of apples
  b 4 lbs.   d 2 lbs.

6 a a bag of flour   b a bag of potatoes   c a watermelon

Comparing and Ordering Mass

Page 216 – Example(s)

b Drawing should have more than 4 marbles.

c Drawing should have more than 3 oranges.

Page 216 – Your Turn

a 3, 2, 1   b 3, 1, 2

Page 217 – Practice

1 a gluestick   c 8   e more   g 36
  b 20   d less   f 8

Mass Review Page 218

1 a Circle item on right.   c Circle item on right.
  b Circle item on left.   d Circle item on right.

2 a Circle both triangles.
  b Check black triangle, cross out red triangle.
  c Check green triangle, cross out red triangle.
  d Circle both triangles.
  e Circle both triangles.
  f Check pink triangle, cross out green triangle.

3 a heavier than   c lighter than
  b the same mass as

4 a 5, 2, 1, 3, 4   b 5, 3, 1, 2, 4   c 5, 1, 2, 3, 4

5 a gluestick   d heavier
  b pencil cas   e 13
  c 3

6 a | 10 kg | 10 kg | 10 kg | 5 kg | 5 kg | 5 kg | 1 kg | 1 kg | 1 kg |
| 10 kg | 10 kg | 10 kg | 5 kg | 5 kg | 5 kg | 1 kg | 1 kg | 1 kg |

b | 10 lbs. | 10 lbs. | 10 lbs. | 5 lbs. | 5 lbs. | 5 lbs. | 1 lb. | 1 lb. | 1 lb. |
| 10 lbs. | 10 lbs. | 10 lbs. | 5 lbs. | 5 lbs. | 5 lbs. | 1 lb. | 1 lb. | 1 lb. |

c | 10 kg | 10 kg | 10 kg | 5 kg | 5 kg | 5 kg | 1 kg | 1 kg | 1 kg |
| 10 kg | 10 kg | 10 kg | 5 kg | 5 kg | 5 kg | 1 kg | 1 kg | 1 kg |

d | 10 lbs. | 10 lbs. | 10 lbs. | 5 lbs. | 5 lbs. | 5 lbs. | 1 lb. | 1 lb. | 1 lb. |
| 10 lbs. | 10 lbs. | 10 lbs. | 5 lbs. | 5 lbs. | 5 lbs. | 1 lb. | 1 lb. | 1 lb. |

7 a 16   b 62   c 57   d 29

8 a twenty-two pounds   d eighty-four kilograms
  b forty-three kilograms   e twenty-one pounds
  c seven pounds

9 a bag of potatoes   b bag of carrots   c bag of rice

13. TIME

Analog Clocks—O'clock and 30

Page 222 – Example(s)
c big, 12
little, 10
10:00 or 10 o'clock

Page 222 – Your Turn
a 7 o'clock or 7:00
b 12:30

Page 223 – Practice
1 a 4 o'clock or 4:00
   b 4:30
   c 2 o'clock or 2:00
   d 12 o'clock or 12:00
   e 3:30

2 a   d   g

   b   e   h

   c   f

Analog Clocks—15 and 45

Page 224 – Example(s)
c big, 3, 15
8:15

Page 224 – Your Turn
a 1:15
b 12:45
c 5:45

Page 225 – Practice
1 a 4:15
   b 11:45
   c 10:15
   d 6:45
   e 10:45

2 a   c   e

   b   d

Five-Minute Intervals

Page 226 – Your Turn
a 3:10
b 3:35

Page 227 – Practice

1 a   c   e

   b   d

2 a 9:35   c 3:05   e 6:10
   b 6:50   d 12:20

3 a 3:15   b 2:55   c 10:25   d 6:40

4 a 1:55   c 8:40   e 3:25   g 2:50
   b 5:20   d 6:35   f 11:10

5 a   b   c

Digital Time

Page 229 – Example(s)
c four fifteen   e six forty-five
d nine ten   f eleven forty

Page 229 – Your Turn
a three fifteen   b two o'clock   c seven thirty-five

Page 230 – Practice
1 a four fifteen   c seven twenty-five   e eight forty
   b five o'clock   d three thirty

2 a 8:30   c 12:00   e 6:45
   b 11:20   d 9:55

3 a one forty   c eleven ten
   b nine o'clock   d twelve fifteen

Time Review Page 231
1 a 2:00   d 1:55   g 3:20
   b 10:25   e 3:45   h 1:00
   c 1:15   f 4:25   i 9:05

2 a 11:35   c 2:10   e 5:50
   b 2:20   d 11:05

3 a two o'clock   e eleven forty-five
   b seven thirty   f four fifty-five
   c twelve thirty-five
   d six fifteen